Kathy Holton
7221 Church Park Dr.
Fort Worth, TX 76133

D0016134

IF CHRIST

WERE YOUR

COUNSELOR

Dr. Chris Thurman

THOMAS NELSON PUBLISHERS
Nashville

All of the characters in the stories are composites of the hundreds of people we have met and talked with during the years of our ministry. Names, genders, and other identifying characteristics have been changed to protect the privacy of those people.

All Scripture quotations are from THE NEW KING JAMES VERSION of the Bible. Copyright © 1979, 1980, 1982, Thomas Nelson, Inc., Publishers.

Published in Nashville, Tennessee, by Janet Thomas Books, a division of Thomas Nelson, Inc., Publishers, and distributed in Canada by Word Communications, Ltd., Richmond, British Columbia, and in the United Kingdom by Word (UK), Ltd., Milton Keynes, England.

Library of Congress Cataloging-in-Publication Data

Thurman, Chris.
    If Christ were your counselor / by Chris Thurman.
      p.   cm.
  ISBN 0-8407-7817-1
    1. Christian life—1960-   2. Jesus Christ—Counseling methods.
I. Title.
BV4501.2.T522   1993
248.4—dc20   93-23871
                                       CIP

Printed in the United States of America
1 2 3 4 5 6 — 98 97 96 95 94 93

To the Counselor of Counselors, Jesus Christ, whose office is never closed and whose heart is always open.

Contents

Acknowledgments

My heartfelt thanks go to the staff at Thomas Nelson Publishers for all the many things they do that make writing a book such a pleasure. Janet Thoma has been such a great source of encouragement to me over the years. She won't settle for less than an author's best, and I appreciate how she has pushed me to grow as a writer with each new book. Sandy Dengler and Kay Strom edited the book and did a fantastic job. They added so many nice touches to what you will read.

I owe a great debt of thanks to Dr. Steve Thurman, Dr. David Ferguson, and Roy Smith for taking time out of their very busy lives to read the first draft of this book and give me much needed feedback. Each of these brothers in Christ provided helpful insights and viewpoints that made a significant contribution to how this book turned out.

My wife, Holly, and children, Matthew, Ashley, and Kelly, are such a joy to me. They help make my life so rich and meaningful. Even though I may have penned the words that you will read, writing this book was a family effort. Holly and the kiddos made it possible for me to work on this book in an atmosphere of love and support that made all the difference in the world.

My clients have taught me more than they will ever know about courage and perseverance. Thank you for blessing me with the honor of being your counselor.

My deepest thanks are to God. The opportunity to write books is just one of many expressions of His grace to me. Anything of value in this book is from Him, not me. Thank you, God, for loving me in an overwhelming way.

Chris Thurman, Ph.D.
Austin, Texas
May 1993

I

Counselor of Counselors

"This also comes from the LORD of hosts,
Who is wonderful in counsel and excellent
in guidance."   Isaiah 28:29

No one will ever say I'm a highly sophisticated connoisseur of art. My idea of fine art is one of those paintings of dogs wearing hats and ties and playing poker, or a rendering of Elvis on velvet. With me, art usually goes in one eye and out the other. Yet, one day while sitting in a colleague's office, I saw a print that made a profound impression on me, one, in fact, that led to the writing of this book.

The print is called "The Divine Counselor" by Harry Anderson, an artist regarded for his religious paintings—especially his works of Christ in modern settings. "The Divine Counselor" portrays Christ in first-century garb, sitting in a twentieth-century office. Brilliant sunshine in the window behind Him provides a dramatic backdrop for the Light of the World, and accents the folds of His white robe. He is intent upon the conversation. His left hand gestures, palm up, as if to say, "You see? The basic principle is simple, though profound." He is talking to a distinguished-looking man in a suit who is seated at a desk. Christ, sitting face-to-face with someone in modern times, engaged in a lively discussion—what I wouldn't give to hear that conversation! My imagination takes over and I let myself picture the details of that scene.

I see the man perhaps as a psychiatrist or psychologist, or a person from any other walk of life, and he and Christ are discussing the nature of people and their problems. I see Christ attempting to enlighten this worldly wise man about what makes people tick, why they develop personal problems, and how those problems can be overcome. A modern counselor or other concerned person getting counseling from the Counselor of Counselors—Wow!

Many today are the counselors and lay people who need this kind of help.

WE HAVE A MESS HERE

Picture the mess in a kitchen after half a dozen first-graders have attempted to bake brownies—broken eggs, spills and splatters, batter dripping into an open flatware drawer, chocolate spots on the curtains and ceiling, and smoke curling out of the oven. The mess in counseling is not so apparent, but that doesn't make it any less real.

One factor contributing to the confusion is that there seems to be as many counseling approaches as there are counselors. Moreover, there is little agreement among counselors themselves as to what competent counseling ought to look like. Some believe that we must go back in time and heal the wounds of childhood, whereas others believe that only our current behavior needs to be addressed. Some counselors believe that finding meaning and purpose in life is important, while others think it necessary to accept yourself and actualize your human potential. In short, ask ten counselors what counseling is supposed to look like, and you are likely to get ten different answers.

Clients become understandably frustrated when the counseling method they choose doesn't seem to really help. And they get downright discouraged and angry when a counselor's advice seems to make things worse. Even more upsetting is to turn from one counselor to another and hear something different from each one. Can you blame the clients for throwing up their hands in disgust, and saying, "It's no use! These people can't even agree among themselves about how to help me. Counseling is nothing but baloney!" While some clients swear by the counsel they receive, too many just swear about the counsel they receive.

MASTERING THE MESS

Clients, then—their satisfaction, healing, and improved lives—are the stakes. If you set the first-graders to work cleaning up the kitchen, the job might eventually get done, sort of. Some kids might be good at getting the stickiness off the floor, but who among them can reach the spots on the ceiling? To do the job efficiently, there must be a single overseer who can point to the floor and also lift little hands up so they can reach the ceiling. A master chef. A linchpin around which the work revolves. An anchor.

While most counseling today is anchored in the theories of counseling "heavyweights" such as Sigmund Freud, B. F. Skinner, Albert Ellis, Carl Rogers, and others, I believe counseling can be truly life-changing *only* if it is anchored in the life and teachings of one person: Jesus Christ.

Why? Christ claimed to be God, and then backed up the claim by living life in a manner that has never been, nor ever will be, matched in human history. Through His life, Christ showed us what perfect maturity in a human being looks like, spending most of His time on earth trying to help people understand how to live life the same way. It is to Him above all others we must pay attention if we really want to understand ourselves, overcome our personal problems, and then help others to do the same.

If you supervise the kitchen cleanup, the utensils will be returned clean to the right places. The flatware will go back to its proper drawer, the mixer beaters to their shelf, and so on. If the children are left to their own devices, a lot of items may be misplaced.

Similarly, Jesus Christ knows where everything goes. It's His kitchen, actually. He was in on our planning and development. He knows what we need in order to experience the abundant life, and He knows how to get us on a healing course when we are deeply troubled. At the human level, no one counselor knows where everything goes, nor even where all the "hiding" places are. Christ knows. No one counselor can say with confidence how to correct every single problem. Christ can.

To master the mess, then, we turn to the Master.

Ah, but what messes could be avoided if we let the Master in on the brownie baking in the first place! Think how great all the brownies would be with His loving and sympathetic supervision. So how do you know if He is in control?

THE CRITERION FOR MESS MANAGEMENT

If you, the reader, are a counselor, or have been in counseling, or have turned to books, tapes, or workshops for help with personal problems, you've heard a lot of different theories about how to master problems. You've been exposed to all manner of suggestions about how to grow as a mature, healthy person. How can you weigh all that advice and pick a reliable course of action that works for you—and, if you are a counselor, for those who trust you?

I suggest that the Master is the measure. What would Jesus Christ, the Counselor of Counselors, tell you? What would He do? Is the counsel with which you are involved in accord with that offered by the greatest counselor of all time? That's what this book is about.

I am convinced that any effort to solve problems is in vain unless it is centered in Christ and His teachings. He is the ultimate criterion for mess management and mess prevention. He is the central figure upon which to anchor every theory, every practice, every thought. With this book I want to hold up for you the measure Christ himself offers, that you may weigh all your problem-solving techniques, counseling methods, therapies, and life-improvement suggestions against the only reliable standard—the Counselor of Counselors.

To see how to do that consistently, let's look back at Harry Anderson's painting, "The Divine Counselor."

PUT YOURSELF IN THE PICTURE

Bring your own imagination into play. Trade places with the man in the picture. Sit in his chair. Listen to what Christ would tell you about your life and about your problems. Here is your chance, through the medium of this book, to go one-on-one with the Counselor of Counselors to see what He has to say about life, liberty, and the pursuit of happiness.

Are you willing? Before you reply, think carefully. Are you willing to put yourself and your life under the counseling microscope of someone who is morally flawless, perfectly discerning, and completely truthful? I think, if you are truly honest with yourself, that your response might be, "Thanks, but I think I'll pass." Who wants to have everything—*everything*—we think, feel, and do placed under the penetrating scrutiny of a human being, much less the God of the universe? A personal encounter with Christ—talking about who we are and how we are living life—would be so painful and embarrassing that many of us would run from it.

Yet, while such an encounter with Christ would be painful, it would be the most freeing experience we could ever have. It would be that once-in-a-lifetime chance to see ourselves as we really are, and to get some help to live life as it was really meant to be lived. It would be an opportunity not to be missed.

Christ has an opening in His counseling schedule. Are you ready to step into His office and hear what He has to say? Ready or not, He just entered the waiting room to greet you.

II

Follow the Real Thing

"First seek the counsel of the LORD."   1 Kings 22:5, NIV

What a crazy, competitive business is the world of advertising! With billions of dollars of revenue on the line each year, advertising agencies have to come up with the catchiest jingles, the most memorable phrases, and the most unforgettable images in order to sell as much of a product as possible. This seems especially true when advertising soft drinks.

"The uncola. Never had it. Never will."

"Uh huh!"

Most phrases come and go. A few stick. One such lasting phrase is Coca Cola's "Coke: It's the real thing!" And listen to the accompanying words in the catchy song: "What the world wants to see; what the world wants to be." What a masterpiece of advertising genius. Regardless of nationality, circumstance, or culture, we all want the real thing.

In a much more important way, we want the real thing when it comes to living life. We want to know what reality is and what it is not. We want to hear from "the authority," not from some inexperienced novice. Unlike the novice, the authority knows all the ins and outs. We need the definitive word regarding the significant matters of life. We need the real thing.

As Christ greets you in the waiting room, I believe His first words to you might be, "Follow me." With those words, He would be saying much more than you might realize. He isn't just asking you to follow Him back to His office; He is asking you to follow *Him*, and only Him, throughout your life. He is letting you know that He is the real thing, and His is the authoritative word on life. In those two simple words, Christ is giving you His most important counsel before you even get to His office.

This is the Good Shepherd who is saying, "Follow me." Now domestic sheep are strange and wonderful animals. Drive a flock at a run over a foot-high barrier and the lead sheep will jump the barrier and continue on, full tilt. The sheep behind will jump it too. Yank the barrier away or let it fall and the rest of the flock will leap just as high at that spot as if the barrier were still there. If the lead sheep mindlessly jumps off a cliff, so will the followers. They'll eat the grass down to a nubbin and then, unless the shepherd leads them to new pastures, stand around and starve to death waiting for more grass to grow.

Scripture does not call human beings sheep for nothing. We follow. If we don't follow the Shepherd, we will follow something else. Following "something else" means "not following the real thing," but with His two simple words, Christ is saying that He is the only trustworthy road map for getting through life. If we follow Him, we will end up where we really want to be. If we follow someone or something else, we will get lost.

THE WRONG ROAD

I got lost. I followed the road map called "humanistic psychology" for a while, and it cost me dearly. Humanistic psychology says that people are basically good, naturally desire to grow, and have the internal resources to resolve their own difficulties. The only problem with this approach to life is that it is full of lies.

Following this human-centered philosophy during my graduate school years took me away from reality: we human beings are not inherently good, we don't really want to work very hard at growing up, and we lack the insight and power necessary to solve our deepest problems. In a very real sense, following the path of humanistic psychology for a number of years took me away from God and, self-destructively, into myself.

When I look around, I see people following many different roads through life other than the one Christ laid out. You can recognize those who are following the road called "materialism," where the motto is, "The person with the most toys wins." You've seen some follow the road called "hedonism," whose motto is, "If it feels good, do it!" Still others follow the road called "relativism": "There are no ultimate truths. You do your thing and I'll do mine." Finally, some follow the road of "pragmatism," where the motto is, "If it works, do it!" There are a few who try to explore all those roads at once, which involves them in a convoluted route through life. Whether we follow these various roads one at a time or in combination, they ultimately poison our souls.

Non-theistic—that is, secular—counselors tell their clients, "Follow me. I'm the real thing. Listen to what I have to say about your problems and how to solve them. I know the best way for you to live your life." They must, of necessity, take over in an authoritative, positive way. But what is the basis of the counseling they offer? To whom are they listening? Where did they obtain their road map for helping people, and why is their method better than anyone else's?

The truth is, most counselors leave school with a hodgepodge of theories, therapies, and techniques under their belt, and they presume that these qualifications are enough to provide competent counsel for their clients. It's all they have. By and large, non-theistic counselors are not concerned with whether or not their approach is consistent with the teachings of the Bible, and they do not use the life of Christ as the ultimate expression of a fully mature person. Because they often leave God and what He has to say out of their thinking as well as out of their work, following these counselors can be dangerous.

And yet, I am equally concerned about what is being touted as "Christian" counseling. I have witnessed many examples of people who claim to offer Christian counseling when, in fact, they offer nothing more than a secular mindset with a Bible verse or two thrown in. The Bible as the source of truth, and the life of Christ as *the* model, are not even mentioned by some of the so-called "Christian" counselors. Unless the ultimate goal of counseling is to help a person become more like Christ, it isn't Christian.

THE RIGHT ROAD

One of my favorite movies is "Hoosiers," starring Gene Hackman. Hackman plays the part of a volatile basketball coach given the task of coaching a high school team in a small Indiana town. Now Indiana is basketball country to the Nth degree, and Hackman receives all kinds of advice from the townspeople as to how best to coach the team. Some of his own players add their two cents worth on how to bring out the best in them. But Hackman has his own strong views as to the best way to mold his players into a winning team, so he ignores all that unsolicited advice.

A pivotal scene comes as the team plays its first game. Complying with Hackman's orders, the team falls behind, much to everyone's dismay. The team is frustrated; the townspeople are yelling from the stands. During the second half, the players decide to ignore the coach's guidance and play the game their way.

In the locker room following the game, Hackman delivers an ultimatum. He says he will not coach players who refuse to play his way. They are told to decide whether they are willing to follow his guidelines or not. Follow him and they can stay on the team. Play their own way, and they're off.

Wisely, the players decide to commit to Hackman's program. Despite being a small school playing larger foes, Hackman guides the team to the state championship. In the face of immense pressure and hostility, from within as well as without, Hackman remained true to his personal convictions because he knew they were right. He knew they would work. Those convictions, coupled with the players' willingness to cooperate, led the team to a level of accomplishment and success that no one had imagined possible.

That film's storyline is the essence of what Christ is trying to do with us. He is the coach trying to get us, the players, to play the game of life the way He knows it can be played best. We, in our immaturity and arrogance, fight His coaching and go our own way. We are swayed by our stubborn desire to run our own lives, and by all those voices up in the stands that yell at us to follow something other than Christ's teachings. Christ allows our rebellion—no one on Hackman's team was forced to play—but He warns us that our way ultimately will fail. His style of play on the court of life will work for us, as long as we commit to doing it His way.

Following any other route than His means we lose. Following Him takes us to new levels of maturity and peace we never would have imagined possible.

"Follow me."

Where to?

The apostle Paul followed Christ so far that he could say, "For to me, to live is Christ, and to die is gain" (Philippians 1:21). What a goal—to follow Christ to such a degree that our very lives are insignificant compared to doing what Christ wants us to do. I'm certainly not there yet, but it is the mark I know is right and one worth pressing toward.

YOUR ROAD

Whom are you following? If it is someone or something other than Christ, you are in deeper trouble than you realize. I fear that all your efforts to be a healthy, mature person are ultimately in vain if they are not anchored in the person of Jesus Christ and in what He says. If you are involved in counseling that does not regard Christ as the centerpiece, I believe you are headed down the wrong road. If, on the other hand, your counseling efforts are based in Christ and in His ability to help, then all things are possible in your efforts to become a complete human being.

The Real Thing has spoken. "Follow me."

Whom are you following?

III

Know Whom You Look Like

"So God created man in His own image . . ." Genesis 1:27

I am convinced my kids look exactly like me. My wife, Holly, thinks they look just like her. Whomever they resemble, I admit they would be a lot better off if they looked like Holly. In reality, though, they look like both of us. We take a great deal of delight in the fact that our children bear "our image." It means something to us that there are three little people on the planet who have our personal stamp, and we hope it means something to them that they resemble us.

It means something to Christ, too. I think, once inside Christ's office, the first item on His agenda would be to work on this issue of whom you look like. This is not a matter of whether you most resemble your father or your mother. It goes much, much deeper. Most of us have rather distorted self images, often alternating between extremes of self-disgust and self-adoration. The "Ain't I awful!" self-disgust we can feel fuels a lot of painful emotions and destructive behavior. The "Ain't I wonderful!" self-adoration feeds our arrogance and pride. Self-disgust and self-adoration, as common as they are, reflect a basic misunderstanding of whom we look like and cripple our efforts to follow Christ down His road.

WHOM WE ARE REALLY LIKE?

If you drive the Interstate 5 corridor from the Canadian border toward Mexico, the first thing you notice is the ubiquitous and vivid green of trees, grass, and moss on roofs and fences. You pass through Seattle with its Annual Rain Festival from January 1 to December 31. In April and May, if you continue south of Portland, you find the constant green broken by acres upon acres of intense yellows, blues, purples, and dazzling whites. These colors are vast fields of iris.

The grower who raises these brilliant flowers spends millions of dollars developing new varieties of iris. But then the grower must beg those new varieties to breed true. That's the hardest part. For unless the new cultivars of irises can maintain their unique traits from generation to generation, with the daughter plants bearing the exact image of the parent plants, they are worth very little. The blankets of joyous color on both sides of the freeway attest to the grower's success. But that success came at a great cost of time and money.

THE IMAGE WE BEAR

So, whom do you resemble? The Captain Gallant, a sturdy iris of burnished copper, imparts its glowing red-brown color to the varieties descended from it. It contributes its strength of stem to the cultivars which would, so to speak, call it "daddy." You too almost certainly share features of your ancestors. Maybe you look like Dad or Mom or Uncle Harry or Aunt Mabel. You might have ended up with your grandmother's freckles or your grandfather's tendency to male pattern baldness. Christ wants us all to fully understand that, beneath the shallow level of the physical, the fundamental image we bear is His.

Whom do you resemble? Him.

Of course, the freckles, the skin color, the receding hairline, the shape of the nose are not what we're talking about here. That we bear God's image means that we share a number of important qualities in common with Him. Dr. Larry Crabb, in his book *Understanding People,* suggests that we resemble God in some key ways, which I've expanded upon.

We, Like God, Have Deep Longings for Close Relationships.

God earnestly wants to be close to us. Listen to the words of Christ in Matthew 23:37: "O Jerusalem, Jerusalem, the one who kills the prophets and stones those who are sent to her! How often I wanted to gather your children together, as a hen gathers her chicks under her wings, but you were not willing!" Hear the depth of God's yearning for relationship in those painfully spoken words!

We bear God's image in that we also have a deep longing (whether we acknowledge it or not) to draw close to Him. As the psalmist put it so beautifully, "My soul thirsts for You;/My flesh longs for You" (Psalm 63:1). We were born to desire a closeness with our Creator, as well as with those whom He created.

We Have the Capacity to Think Evaluatively.

At the county fair, the farmers display a wonderful array of produce in competition for the grand prize. Quilts are judged over in the Home Arts hall. The Future Farmers and 4–H kids trot out their best livestock and vegetables, hoping for a ribbon. Which farmer's booth is best? Which quilt? Which sheep or pumpkin? Evaluation. And after the judging is done, you may not agree with the choices. After all, you have your own standards of evaluation, just as the judges do.

When Christ was in this world, He frequently evaluated people's lives—their thoughts, motives, feelings, and actions. He did so, not to shame or humiliate them, but to show them the self-destructive path they were on so they could turn from it. We, like God, have that capacity to evaluate people, situations, ourselves. Unlike God, though, our capacity for fair, objective, honest evaluation of self and others has been greatly diminished by sin. We can't make evaluations with anything like the same level of honesty and objectivity that God can. God, in Isaiah 55:8, puts it this way: "My thoughts are not your thoughts."

We, Like God, Exercise Free Will.

In order to get his new varieties breeding true, the iris grower must experiment with crosses and genetics over several generations. Children of God can "breed true," taking on the attributes of the Father within their own generation, for the likeness is governed, not by heredity, but by obedience.

God does whatever He wants to do, and His actions are directed by the ". . . mystery of His will" (See Ephesians 1:9). "I will be gracious to whom I will be gracious, and I will have compassion on whom I will have compassion" (Exodus 33:19). We are free to do whatever we wish, and our actions are directed by our own will. How God uses His will and how we often use ours, though, are much different. God uses His will to love us and bring us to maturity. We often use our wills to act unlovingly and to drift into immaturity. Left to our own devices, we would frequently use our wills to hurt others and even ourselves. Therefore God strongly encourages us in Philippians 2:13 to allow Him to work through us "to will and to do for His good pleasure." We greatly need God's help to use our wills to be loving and mature.

Like God, We Experience Emotions.

"Then the anger of the LORD was aroused against Israel" (2 Kings 13:3). God got mad! "Have mercy upon me, O God,/According to Your lovingkindness" (Psalm 51:1). "Do good in Your good pleasure to Zion;/. . . Then You shall be pleased with the sacrifices of righteousness" (Psalm 51:18, 19). Christ wept when Lazarus died (see John 11:33–36), reacted in anger at the money lenders in the temple (see John 2:14–17), and became so grieved about taking the sins of the world on His shoulders that He said, "My soul is exceedingly sorrowful, even to death" (Matthew 26:38). Simply put, God experiences the full range of powerful emotions, as do we. God's emotions, though, are always perfectly in tune with the situation He is facing, whereas all too often our emotions are not.

Like God, We Are Spiritual Beings.

He is spirit, of course. Scripture says so. By possessing a spiritual dimension (and Scripture says that, too!), we share His nature, His most intimate being. Thus, we thirst for our Creator and long to be like Him. Our spirit enables us to interact with God and know we are His. As Paul said, "The Spirit Himself bears witness to our spirit that we are children of God" (Romans 8:16).

We bear His image, then, in that He put these five characteristics, or qualities, into us. They are His way of saying we are His children before we are anyone else's. That's right; you are God's child before you are your parents'! However close our human family resemblances, we actually look more like God than we do our parents, and our children look more like God than they do us.

It is important to remember before going too much further how we do *not* resemble God. We are not omnipotent (all powerful), omniscient (all knowing), or omnipresent (everywhere at once), as is He. We would love to be like God in these ways. Many of us play God in these three ways and then are frustrated to find He didn't put these qualities into us. We try in vain to know it all, to do everything, to be everywhere at once.

You may have seen the poster that identifies two truths in life: 1) There is a God; 2) You are not He. As that great philosopher Clint Eastwood used to say in the Dirty Harry films, "A man has to know his limitations." God wants you to know that you are a "fearfully and wonderfully made" (Psalm 139:14) reproduction of Him, but you are not by any stretch of the imagination the original! I think we can live with that.

THE PRACTICAL ASPECT OF BEARING HIS IMAGE

Why would Christ focus on "His image" in His efforts to counsel you? Because He knows that how you view yourself significantly impacts how you live your life. He knows that if we think we look like something or someone other than Him, we will have a problem of self-image that leads us into misery and sin.

From Scripture, I can see what Christ the Counselor wants you to know about your self-worth. You can neither raise nor lower your self-worth because it is based in being, not doing. You were created "a little lower than the angels" and crowned "with glory and honor" (Psalm 8:5). You can't top that if you try!

You cannot, therefore, have more self-worth tomorrow than you have today—or less—because you will always be an image bearer. Improve your worth? You can't. All you can do is recognize the completeness of it and avoid the trap of trying to become worthier by doing something better.

Imagine for a moment that every one of the five billion people on this planet is a car. Each car is unique—different make, different model. The way many of us try to find self-worth is by comparing our cars with other people's and hoping that ours will come out on top. If my car is sleeker and faster than yours, I feel superior to you and good about myself. Of course, if my car compares poorly— boxy, not-too-bright, slower, unappealing—I feel inferior to you and not very good about myself. When we compare ourselves to others, as we might compare vehicles, we usually end up with feeling superior, inferior, or even both at once. These destructive feelings prevent us from seeing how much we resemble others, and from growing closer to them. True intimacy is lost.

In this initial session, Christ would have you know that one thing, and one thing only, imbues your car with worth—His name stamped on the bumper. That is enough.

Much of secular counseling takes a significantly different approach to the issue of self-worth than that which Christ would propose to you. Non-theistic counsel usually points out that you have worth because you are. You exist. That is enough. Now, counselors might say, go improve your worth by "being your own best friend," "winning through intimidation," "looking out for number one," "pulling your own strings."

Solomon in the book of Ecclesiastes lets us know that he tried that route—and outdid everyone else at it—and his life ended up being nothing more than a sham because God was not at the center of it. Here was a man envied as much as any figure in history, yet he was probably one of the most miserable.

Enviable? Solomon had seven hundred wives, three hundred concubines, and wealth beyond reckoning. He had the richest, most delectable food in the world, provided by the farms of one of that era's greatest agricultural regions. He also enjoyed respite from his enemies for his warrior father, David, had vanquished the nation's foes. Solomon wrote extensively about natural history seven hundred years before Aristotle (see 1 Kings 4:33). He wrote songs. He compiled his nation's proverbs, and coined quite a few of his own. He garnered immense fame and respect for his consummate wisdom. Kings and queens stood in awe of him. Enviable! Yet he moaned in Ecclesiastes, "Vanity of vanities, all is vanity" (1:2). His wisdom rings through the ages, but achieving success the way the world defines it, does nothing lasting for self-worth.

So Christ would tell you that if you have a self-worth problem, you are looking at yourself through distorted eyewear. You are seeing yourself as better or worse than you are, or both, and you are using performance as the way to improve that image.

I'M FREE!

Of what value is this whole matter of self-worth and self-image, anyway? Much indeed! The fact that we look like God in all the ways that really matter can solve the nagging problem most of us have: being obsessed with ourselves and using performance to try to like ourselves more. Eliminating that self-obsession frees us up to be more available to God. As A. W. Tozier said in *Man the Dwelling Place of God,* "The victorious Christian neither exalts nor downgrades himself. His interest has shifted from self to Christ. What he is or is not no longer concerns him. He believes that he has been crucified with Christ and he is not willing either to praise or deprecate such a man."

So while you may have your earthly dad's nose, or your earthly mom's hair color, you look more like God than anyone else. You are God's child, an incredible reproduction of the original.

There is joy in Salem, Oregon, when a dazzling new iris cultivar breeds true, reproducing the gorgeous image from generation to generation, and the world is enriched by another beautiful variety of flower. Infinitely moreso does God experience great joy in the fact that we bear His image. He wants us to have that same joy as well.

Most of us don't have that joy, though, because most of us don't know we look like Him. Not understanding that we are image bearers, we seek worth we already have. What a waste of time, effort, and talent! There are few things sadder than spending our lives not knowing we already have great value, and all because we don't know how wonderful it is to bear God's image. It's one of the most grievous mistakes we can make. I know, because that is one of the mistakes I have made. I don't know many people who haven't.

Let me ask you a very important question. Do you know who you look like? Make sure you do! The quality of your life hinges upon how well you answer that question.

IV

Live Like an Heir

"Therefore you are no longer a slave but a son; and if a son, then an heir of God through Christ." Galatians 4:7

Smitten by love, a young Englishman, Captain Cedric Errol, married an American woman. Infuriated, his wealthy father, the Earl of Dorincourt, promptly and summarily disinherited him. Captain Errol and his wife faced a bleak future in England; after all, even had he not been disinherited, Cedric was the third son, and certainly not in line for any major windfalls. So the couple moved to America and there built a modest life for themselves. In America, they had their first and only child, Cedric, Jr. Unfortunately, Captain Errol died prematurely, leaving his wife and young Cedric to face the world together, in poverty.

Victorian romance to the rescue! Cedric was seven years old when Mr. Havisham, the family lawyer for the Earl of Dorincourt, arrived on the doorstep. Mr. Havisham informed Cedric and his mother that the Earl of Dorincourt's two oldest sons had died, leaving only Cedric to inherit the family fortune. Cedric, as the Earl of Dorincourt's only grandchild, is now the sole heir to the great wealth and power of the earldom. Cedric, now Lord Fauntleroy, is escorted to England that he might eventually assume his responsibilities as Earl of Dorincourt.

Mr. Havisham, in his initial meetings with the boy, saw that Cedric "had not the least idea of the sort of thing he was to see when he reached England, or the sort of home that waited for him there." So, he attempted to help Cedric and his mother understand some of the privileges that would accompany his position as Lord Fauntleroy. Before leaving for England to live under his grandfather's roof, Cedric uses some of his inheritance to do a variety of helpful things for the people in his life that he loves. He reaches out with great sensitivity and kindness, lovingly taking care of the many needs he sees around him.

Yet, while Cedric is allowed to use some of his grandfather's wealth as he pleases in America, the full extent of his privileges as Lord Fauntleroy have to wait until he is living in England with his grandfather. While in America, Cedric gets only a small taste of his grandfather's wealth, but in England, he will see exactly what it means to be Lord Fauntleroy.

Little Lord Fauntleroy, written in 1886 by Frances Hodgson Burnett, is the touching story of how a young American boy's life is turned upside down when he becomes the sole heir to a vast fortune in England. Even though the book did not specifically offer a spiritual perspective, *Little Lord Fauntleroy* holds some very important clues as to how we, as Christians, ought to live our lives.

As Christ continues in His efforts to counsel you, I think He would focus on the central theme that Frances Hodgson Burnett used in writing *Little Lord Fauntleroy* to help you find victory in your day-to-day struggles.

CONGRATULATIONS! YOU ARE NOBILITY!

Understanding this central theme is critical if we are to live life with the power, honor, and glory that we are meant to. The central theme is this: You, as a Christian, are now the heir to God's vast fortune, and you have all the rights and privileges that go with being His heir.

When you became a Christian, you were spiritually reborn and became a child of God. As a child of God, you are now an heir to all that He has. You are a member of a spiritual nobility. Here is just a short list of what happened when you became a child of God. It will remain true forever:

- You were justified and redeemed. (See Romans 3:24.)
- You were sanctified (made holy, set apart). (See 1 Corinthians 1:2.)
- You were set free from the law of sin and death. (See Romans 8:2.)
- You were sealed with the Holy Spirit. (See Ephesians 1:13.)
- You were given access to God. (See Ephesians 3:12.)
- You were brought out of darkness into the light. (See Ephesians 5:8.)
- All your needs were supplied. (See Philippians 4:19.)
- You were made complete. (See Colossians 2:10.)
- Your life was hidden with Christ in God. (See Colossians 3:3.)
- Your heart and mind were guarded by the peace of God. (See Philippians 4:7.)
- You were accepted. (See Romans 15:7.)
- You were made into a new creature. (See 2 Corinthians 5:17.)
- You were forgiven. (See Ephesians 1:7.)
- You were seated in heaven. (See Ephesians 2:6.)
- You were made a member of His body. (See Ephesians 5:30.)
- You were given an inheritance. (See Ephesians 1:10–11.)
- You were liberated. (See Galatians 2:4.)
- You were brought near to God. (See Ephesians 2:13.)

As a Christian, you are no longer a person of dishonor but a person of honor. You are no longer powerless but powerful through God. Your life is no longer hopeless but hopeful. Regardless of how bleak your past may have been, you have an incredibly bright future. Incredible things about you and your situation changed when you turned your life over to Christ.

AND THAT'S NOT ALL!

Little Lord Fauntleroy illustrates other important parallels as well. Similar to the situation in which Lord Fauntleroy found himself, we are not home yet and thus are unable to fully exercise or enjoy our privileges as heirs. We are still in Cedric's America in that we live on earth, and Cedric's England, our home in heaven and the site of our actual earldom, is yet to come. While here, we look forward to the day when we reach heaven and obtain our full inheritance. Until that day, we face the limitations of being in a fallen world in a human body, battling our own and other people's selfishness. And then, of course, there is death.

If you were a Christian living in Rome during the reign of Diocletian, you would find yourself persecuted for your faith. You would also be a member of a vibrant, growing church. Some of the disadvantages: Diocletian ordered Christians to be tortured, hung upside down from a stake and burned, drowned, and buried alive. Archers were to shoot Sebastian of Nevarre, but when he survived the arrows, they clubbed him to death.

To see the advantages of living during Diocletian's reign, though, you had only to walk south of Rome on the Appian Way. You would pass the Colosseum and the sumptuous new public baths, adorned with vivid tiles, mosaics, and statuary. You would leave the city through the gate called the Dripping Arch, so named because no matter how the engineers tried, they could not seal a leaking aqueduct. South of the gate for miles along both sides of the road, you would pass the tombs of the wealthy. And the inscriptions on those tombs would show you instantly the value of the Christian walk.

"As you pass, Stranger, reflect on the futility of life."

"A short life, a painful death, and oblivion."

"Who remembers me? Nobody. I am dust."

These were the people who counted most in Roman society, the cream of the cream. Oblivion. Dust. Futility. Before long you would come to an intricate honeycomb of caves. Some of the caves occurred naturally. Many were enlarged into chambers with ante-rooms. Others were hewn anew from the soft, crumbling rock. In these caves, the Catacombs, Christians could hide because the superstitious Romans refused to go in. Christians could put aside superstition; they had something infinitely better. Here the Christians buried their dead.

"Gone to glory."

"Jesus, remember me."

The sign of the fish; the universal badge of recognition.

In the dancing light of the Italian sun, loss and dismay are apparent on every tomb. In the dank gloom of narrow tunnels, hope and peace abound. Our lives would be horribly bleak if it weren't for the fact that we know we are going home to heaven some day.

What's more, we have God's help to live meaningful lives here on earth before we go. Our Father in heaven shares marvelous tidbits of His fortune with us while we are here. Paul, writing to the Philippians, put it this way: "For I am hard pressed between the two, having a desire to depart and be with Christ, which is far better. Nevertheless to remain in the flesh is more needful for you" (Philippians 1:23–24). In other words, Paul wanted to go home to enjoy the awesome gift of being with Christ in heaven more than stay here on earth, but he was willing to stay on earth and do God's will until God was ready to take him home.

If we are seeing things properly, this deep conviction of Paul's will be ours as well. We really are, as one person put it, spending "a bad night in a cheap hotel" while here on earth, but it is here on earth that God wants our service until the proper time comes.

Little Lord Fauntleroy didn't have any idea what would be expected of him. His mentor, Havisham, knew that the lad required some long and grueling preparation. So do we. We prepare by staying here as long as God wants us to, and using our time here for His glory. And we do so, knowing that so much more is waiting for us in heaven. Most probably Cedric didn't have any better notion of what life as an English earl would be like than we have of heaven's glories. The monies supplied to him in America, grand as they seemed to him, were nothing compared with the wealth waiting for him across the sea.

The implication of all this is truly life-changing. We are to live our lives as the heirs to God's fortune. Riches we can't even fathom are already ours and waiting for us! We are to shed the "poor American boy" mindset and deeply embrace the "wealthy English lord" mindset. Cedric did not immediately begin to behave pompously and arrogantly. He served, and cared, and helped. He distributed to others the fortune that had fallen upon him. As should we.

We are new creatures in Christ and need to behave as such. Everything of true value is ours right now even if we are not able to enjoy it all fully at the moment.

Many Christians, myself included, struggle with making the transition from a worldly to a heavenly mindset. In our ignorance about the riches of God's kingdom, we often pursue earthly imitations of heaven as though they were more important and valuable. We settle for less here on earth when there is so much more. C. S. Lewis, in his book *The Weight of Glory and Other Addresses,* powerfully states it this way: "We are half-hearted creatures fooling around with drink and sex and ambition when infinite joy is offered us, like an ignorant child who wants to go on making mud pies in a slum because he cannot imagine what is meant by the offer of a holiday at the sea. We are far too easily pleased."

Little Lord Fauntleroy could have kept on making mud pies instead of accepting his grandfather's call to come live with him. He could have refused to accept his place in the Dorincourt house, and turned down all the privileges that went with it. He could have said, "Sorry. I'd rather be Cedric Errol here in America than Lord Fauntleroy over in England. Besides, I don't want to be reconciled with my family. I don't really know them. I'll hang out here with my friends."

But he didn't, of course, and everything in his life turned out so much better. As a consequence, his friends' fortunes improved as well.

The story of Little Lord Fauntleroy isn't a perfect analogy of our relationship with our heavenly Father. The Earl of Dorincourt disinherited his son. God will never disinherit His children, regardless of what they do. Further, the Earl of Dorincourt was a "selfish and self-indulgent and arrogant" man who "had a cruel tongue and a bitter nature, and he took pleasure in sneering at people and making them feel uncomfortable, when he had the power to do so, because they were sensitive or proud or timid." Your heavenly Father is none of those things. God couldn't love you more, and everything He does toward you is done with your best interest in mind. His plans are to help you, not to harm you. Finally, when Little Lord Fauntleroy inherited the earldom, the story emphasized the increased financial wealth that came with the title, whereas the emphasis in God's kingdom is on how being God's heir increases our spiritual wealth.

So, while here on earth, live like an heir. Never settle for mud pies when you can have a holiday at the sea.

Are you living like an orphan or like the heir that you are?

V

Clean the Inside of the Cup

"Woe to you, scribes and Pharisees, hypocrites! For you cleanse the outside of the cup and dish, but inside they are full of extortion and self-indulgence. Blind Pharisee, first cleanse the inside of the cup and dish, that the outside of them may be clean also." Matthew 23:25–26

Three times in a row, Larry's neighbor's ponies got out on the road. It was time to fix the fence. Unfortunately, it was also that time last winter when all the miserably cold, rainy weather was engulfing Texas. Nevertheless, Larry put on his old barn boots, a couple layers of beat-up sweats, a rain slicker and his *really* beat-up, *really* old Stetson.

Drafted to help him, Hank, Larry's business colleague and neighbor next door, dressed in even grungier clothes. Hank's black wool knitted watch cap kept his head warm, sort of, but you had to ignore the moth holes and faded spots. His pants and gloves had so many grease stains they were on the Environmental Protection Agency's #1 hit list.

Larry and Hank spent one whole Saturday out setting steel posts and stretching wire, slopping in the slop, hunkering in the rain, getting cold as an Eskimo's lawnmower. The fence built and darkness upon them, Larry and Hank slogged gracelessly to the house for hot food and a soft chair. They were wet, muddy, and bedraggled.

A week later, as Hank described the scene to me, he laughed.

"Tell me! What business client in his right mind would ever trust the financial counsel of a pair of bozos who looked like *that?!*"

And he was right! They presented the image of two losers. Why, it was obvious they weren't even smart enough to come in out of the rain. Their images were tarnished.

In America, image is everything. We devote much time and effort to changing external behavior and appearances instead of focusing on improving our internal behavior—our character. In our culture it is more important to look mature than to be mature, to act morally than to be moral. How many people who appear to care actually do care?

Look at the Clinton-Bush presidential campaign. Both parties employed armies of "personality polishers" and spin doctors. Image-makers don't come cheap. The televised debates, particularly that town meeting forum, relied almost exclusively on image, rather than on presenting an honest look at who those men really were beneath the surface.

Yet, before we get too critical of those running for public office, we might admit that we are all politicians. We all present an image to others that isn't totally real. To some degree, we all get caught up in image maintenance, and we go to great lengths to avoid letting other people see us as we really are. I call it the Color Game.

LEAPING LIZARDS!

Set certain lizards—the African chameleon or the American chameleon of our Southeast—on a green background, and within a minute or two, their skins will turn green. Move them to a brown background and their green will fade and turn brown. They pull off the trick by concealing certain pigmented cells and exposing others. It's a safety ploy to make them less obvious and therefore less likely to be grabbed by predators.

In the Color Game the object is not just to avoid harm, but to gain approval. To accomplish this, we figure out people's "color"—who they are, what they like and don't like, what they value—and we become that color. Like chameleons, we blend into the interpersonal terrain so that people will not respond to us in negative ways. If all goes well, people will respond to us in positive ways, and this will serve as our reward and encourage us to continue to play.

Were we living the simple, though hazardous, life of a lizard, playing the Color Game would pose few problems. But we are us, and the advantages and disadvantages of the game cancel themselves out.

First, it's quite a challenge to accurately read another person's color. And there are so many colors. Generally, lizards choose between green and brown. Real people present a rainbow. We constantly feel anxious about assessing a person's color and then changing to fit it.

Second, even if we successfully become what someone else wants us to be, and gain their approval, we are under pressure to keep up the color change in order to maintain that approval. What if that person discovers it's a sham? Stress city! And when we lizards leap quickly and frequently from one environment to another, as when dealing with first one person and then someone else, or moving from the board room to the lunch room to the fitness center, we have to shift colors rapidly.

Third, even when we win that coveted approval, it doesn't really feel good. It's not us those people like, it's the color we became. They approved a certain image, not the real us.

And finally, in the broader sense, this whole shallow game of manipulation kills any chance of true intimacy. When people erect masks, hiding what they don't want the world to see, they hide their true selves. Genuine intimacy develops only when people are being real with one another. How can A know and understand the real B if A cannot see the real B?

So we shift shades, hoping others will approve of us, but not really enjoying it when they do. If we play the game long enough, we lose touch with our original color and our uniqueness. We no longer know for certain what we think, believe, value, and need.

WHAT COLOR IS YOUR COUNSELOR?

Your Counselor knows all about the Color Game. When He walked the earth, He was constantly accosted by people who wanted Him to become something other than what He was. When you come to think about it, it was one of His stronger temptations. Some expected Him to be a military messiah who would gather an army and use brute force to throw out the hated Romans.

Others wanted Him to be a guy who would play by all the current rules of His day and who would fit into the system as it was. Still others wanted Him to just go away.

But Christ stayed true to His hue. He was the Servant Savior. Period. "For even the Son of Man did not come to be served, but to serve, and to give His life a ransom for many" (Mark 10:45). No call to arms, no glorious military campaign, no change of color to win anyone's approval. Some became so angry about His unwillingness to change colors that they nailed him to a tree.

As you sit in Christ's counseling office, He wants you to understand that you face much the same challenges He did. You were created a very special person. Yet, a lot of people may not like you; you don't fit into their preconceived mold. Still, there is no one else on earth exactly like you, and you must be true to the person God made.

Easier said than done, right?

Of all people, I know that. Most of my thirty-nine years have been spent changing color so people would like me. That approval felt good! But it never filled the hole in my soul that ached to be filled. When I "won" someone's approval, I "lost" because I cheapened my own existence.

Yet, to be myself scares the starch out of me sometimes. I am not talking about someone getting wet and muddy in grubby clothes, like Hank and Larry. That's external. It's easy to laugh about something like that, and even easier to fix—a hot shower and clean clothes quickly create a shiny new image. I'm talking about the real me, inside. If I reveal the true me, you might not like what you see. You might even notice some hideous things, things that merit the strongest disapproval. That hurts! Still, I know that Christ would rather see me experience painful rejection by being real than gain artificial acceptance by playing a role. He never compromised, never played the role. Neither should you or I.

How can you put the Color Game aside?

ABANDONING THE COLOR GAME

Heaven knows, Paul tried! The beleaguered apostle sooner or later found himself at odds with Barnabas, with his protégé, Mark, with many of the churches he founded, and with the Roman army. He argued with Peter, of all people—and won. The men of Beroea diligently searched the Scriptures, checking up on him to make certain he was preaching the truth. He was beaten, stoned, imprisoned, shipwrecked, and snakebitten. It's enough to make you want to quit this apostle business and take up some nice, quiet occupation, like lion hunting.

But through it all, Paul remained his own man. Through thick and thin he stayed true to the hue. In fact, that's what got him into trouble more than once. So how is it that this obstinate, powerful, saintly curmudgeon would write, "For though I am free from all men, I have made myself a servant to all, that I might win the more. And to the Jews I became as a Jew, that I might win Jews; to those who are under the law, as under the law, that I might win those who are under the law; to those who are without law, as without law (not being without law toward God, but under law toward Christ), that I might win those who are without law; to the weak I became as weak, that I might win the weak. I have become all things to all men, that I might by all means save some. Now this I do for the gospel's sake, that I may be partaker of it with you" (1 Corinthians 9:19–23).

Does it look like the Color Game? Look again. What was Paul's goal? The gospel. "I do it for the gospel's sake." He was not out for approval. In fact, he often experienced rejection and disapproval from Christians as well as others. In order to win people to Christ, he started where they were, walking in their shoes, and then led them around to his point of view. Always he returned to his position. As you read his biographical material in Acts and his letters later on, you can see he never compromised his beliefs. (Read about his argument with Peter in Galatians 2:11–21. This was a pillar of the church that Paul was raining all over!)

Paul successfully walked the very fine line between caring about others and playing the Color Game. He understood those people whose beliefs were not his, yet he wanted them to move beyond their beliefs into eternal life. He loved them.

So does Jesus.

Your Counselor would say that this is the time to stop and work on the inside of the cup. It is time to face up to who we really are, even if it hurts to do so, and to work on our character rather than our image. Does all this pain and struggle, this refusal to play the Color Game, provide some reward? Absolutely!

First, you find out who your real friends are. Refusal to play the game separates those who are on your side and those who are not. Your "fair weather" friends will drop by the wayside because they really don't want you to be you. That's rejection of the deepest kind, and it hurts, especially if you've been working hard to win *everyone's* approval. Your true friends, though, will stick around. They will love the real you, and that is approval of the highest kind. They may not always like your color but they are committed to loving you. That is a friend, indeed.

Second, you rediscover the freedom inherent in being who you are. This came home to me in a very real way when the daughter of an old friend talked about her wedding plans.

"What I'd really love," she said, "is a quiet little wedding with close friends, and then a big, happy, picnic-type reception afterwards. Neither my fiancé nor I like those super-splash weddings with five hundred guests."

"So what's the problem?" her father asked. "Finances?"

"Oh, we have the money to have any kind of wedding we want. That's not it. It's just that, well, my friends at school say I ought to have a big blowout. It's only going to happen once, you know. And some of the older people in the church don't think that what we have in mind is proper. You know, it just isn't done."

"What? You're going to dance down the aisle in a red leotard and throw rice pudding at all the guests who were planning to throw rice at you?"

She giggled. "No. You know what I mean. You're supposed to have a spray of flowers on every pew, and a ring bearer, and a flower girl and all that kind of thing."

"Who's getting married? Your school buddies and all those older people?"

"I am, but . . ."

"And whom do you strive to please?"

"Jesus, actually. And my fiancé, of course. And . . ."

"I repeat. What's the problem?"

To her father's delight, she caught his meaning and ran with it. She and her fiancé put together a wedding to please each other. They made the ceremony itself very simple and very expressive. She wore a white gown, reflecting Spanish nobility of two hundred years before, with a long white lace mantilla in place of a veil. He wore a white suit—western cut, with the flared cuffs of the Spanish dons, reflecting the New Mexico country where he grew up. The bridesmaids appeared in dusky rose and turquoise western-cut dresses. The effect was stunning. In the ceremony, they both paid public testimony to the role of Jesus Christ in their lives.

Although they would have preferred to keep the guest list short, they let it burgeon at their mothers' request. It seemed to them that the world had been invited, but they allowed that the world thereby heard their commitment to Jesus Christ. Besides, they admitted, being surrounded by lots of friends added to the occasion.

And the reception! Beef slow-barbecued on a spit, chili, beans, rice, corn-on-the-cob, and great plump loaves of sourdough bread. An up-and-coming country-western band played both old favorites and new songs. The Inaugural Ball at the White House couldn't have been more fun.

Whether the older people clucked and wagged their heads I don't know. I do know this girl and her husband revealed their true selves—two easy-going, informal young people devoted to their Lord—and it was beautiful.

Once you get past the need to be liked by all, you can interact with people as you are. When you quit playing the game, you are free of a tremendous burden.

Finally, and most importantly, you become more focused on pleasing God. Paul, as usual, said it well: "For do I now persuade men, or God? Or do I seek to please men? For if I still pleased men, I would not be a bondservant of Christ" (Galatians 1:10).

We want to please God, not because He'll like us better—He already loves us totally—but because of His gifts given to us already. To please God is to please the right person. Giving up our need to please people allows us to focus more clearly on meeting God's desires for our lives, and is a way of saying "thanks" for all He has done for us. His statement about Christ, "This is My beloved son, in whom I am well pleased" is the one statement we *really* want to hear Him say about us (See Matthew 3:17).

So, are you working on polishing up your external image, or are you working on changing your internal character? Are you focusing on losing weight, or are you dealing with the internal issues that cause you to overeat? Are you trying to get along better with your spouse, or are you taking an honest look at why you have difficulty truly loving someone? Are you trying to be more successful in the world, or are you examining why you base your sense of worth on worldly success? Christ, in His loving way, would challenge you to focus on your internal character first. As hard as it is to do, this is where true change and maturity must take place.

Ultimately, internal changes show up on the outside. God made us that way so that people will notice and ask, "How did that happen?" When they ask us about why we are different, we are supposed to point our finger upward and say, "Him." Self-glory is not the purpose of trying to mature. Our lives and the changes we make with God's help are supposed to point people back to the Father.

Are you working on the inside of the cup?

VI

Let Others Off the Hook

"And be kind to one another, tenderhearted, forgiving one another, even as God in Christ forgave you." Ephesians 4:32

Joe and his old college roommate, Mack, decided to go into business together. By pooling their resources, they bought the necessary licenses, permits, corporation papers, and two eighteen-wheelers—a flatbed and a refrigerator truck. Their trucking fleet grew to four rigs, and then seven. They could haul just about anything, and at a good price, too. When they bought a logging truck to haul pine, Joe handled the home office in Houston, and Mac moved east to direct a new center of operations.

Everything was going well until federal agents walked into Joe's office one morning and arrested him.

Unbeknown to Joe, Mack had been using the trucking company to haul illegal drugs. It ruined his reputation and his business. Joe was clean, absolutely clean, but his company had now been involved in illegal activities, and he had to hire an expensive lawyer to get him off the hook. After a long legal battle, the lawyer managed to clear him, but the DEA confiscated all the company's trucks. By the time the lawyer got five of them back (the other three, caught red-handed, so to speak, never were returned), Joe could just about have bought new ones. He filed for bankruptcy.

It was a spectacular case. Not spectacular at all, but every bit as devastating, was the matter of a woman we will call Anne who, as a child, had been sexually abused by her father and her older stepbrother. She was an emergency room nurse, or rather she was try-ing to be, but whenever any sexual abuse or sexual assault victims were brought in, Anne turned into an emotional wreck for the rest of her shift.

What Joe and Anne both yearned for was a magic pill that could be taken to heal the pain—an aspirin for the soul. They needed a nostrum that would soothe the hatred and bitterness inside. Unfortu-nately, there is no such drug.

Joe and Anne both turned to counseling in an effort to overcome the hatred and bitterness they felt toward the people who had caused them such misery. I was the counselor they chose. My work was really cut out for me this time, for they had an enormous amount of pain to overcome.

Both began by telling me their stories. They described the pain they still felt over what had happened to them. I listened as the in-cest victim related how her father used to come home early from work, before the mother returned from her job, and force Anne to have sexual intercourse with him. Her stepbrother loved to ambush her, catching her in the garage, or when she took the trash out after dark. Can you imagine how it felt, growing up in that house?

I listened as Joe related how his crooked partner had ruined ten years of his life. I listened as he talked about how he was finding it nearly impossible to pick up the pieces again, years after the ax had fallen.

As I listened to them, I felt nearly as helpless as they. It seemed I had so little to say that could really make a difference. Yet, I knew that what they needed initially was simply for me to listen. And I did.

After we have listened, though, what do we do to help? How do we proceed with the business of assisting someone through such horrible events as these? What is supposed to be the aim of our efforts with someone who has experienced something that unfairly tears them and their world apart? There is a medicine, but it is con-stantly misused.

THE MISUNDERSTOOD MEDICINE

A man convicted of murdering a young woman was given a moderate, second-degree sentence. If he behaved himself, he would be eligible for parole in approximately seven years. Routine, in this day and age. The trial venue was nearly four hundred miles from the prison, where he would serve his time, so the sheriff decided to transport him by air. Also routine. Video cameras were on hand at the small local airport to film his departure. Routine, for a slow news day.

As the convict, accompanied by a deputy, was walking through the airport in his manacles and ankle chains (also routine), a man at a nearby pay phone suddenly dropped the receiver, walked quickly forward, placed a gun at the convict's head and pulled the trigger. The prisoner died instantly at the deputy's feet. And the video cameras rolled on.

The man who shot the convicted killer was the father of the young woman he had killed.

Hardly a routine turn of events, but the reaction most people felt when they heard about it was, in a sense, routine. It certainly was common; it was the father, now a murderer himself, who received the public sympathy and support. That father's anguished response strikes a very familiar chord in so many of us. A lot of us have felt the same sort of vindictiveness as did the father who gunned down his daughter's murderer, if not to the same degree.

There is a medicine. Forgiveness. And it is so misunderstood that it is either ignored or ridiculed. Try to explain to Anne or Joe about the medicine of forgiveness they need.

Forgiveness. And it seems not only impossible to forgive someone who has done a great wrong to us, but it seems illogical. It is the last thing we feel like doing. When wronged, our hearts immediately hate the wrongdoer and withhold forgiveness as a way of getting back. We want that wrongdoer to suffer as badly as we have suffered.

Sometimes, when it appears the villain is going to escape relatively unscathed, and it seems that no one will step forward to champion justice, we take vengeance into our own hands.

What is the fruit of that? Anne and Joe let their souls shrivel, and there seemed to be nothing they could do to bring themselves back to health. They shared the depressing thought that retribution for the wrongdoers was remote. The possibility of either Anne or Joe forgiving these people was nonexistent.

One of the concepts I had to help Anne and Joe grasp was that vengeance is not ours. It never has been.

Vengeance Is Not Yours, Saith the Lord.

David learned that lesson from a beautiful, intelligent, and virtuous woman called Abigail, who just happened to be married to a supreme loser. When Abigail's husband, Nabal, slighted David's messengers and insulted him, David vowed vengeance. With four hundred crack soldiers, he headed toward Nabal's farm. Abigail quickly produced a sumptuous gift, intercepted David, praised him to the skies, presented her gift, advising him in the strongest terms to refrain from bloodshed—her husband's blood, of course.

David took the divine hint. He recognized where her advice came from. As he put it, "Blessed be the LORD God of Israel, who sent you this day to meet me! And blessed is your advice and blessed are you, because you have kept me this day from coming to bloodshed and from avenging myself with my own hand" (1 Samuel 25:32–33). He accepted her gift and sent her home in peace.

When Abigail got home, the husband, whose life she had just saved, was drunk. So she waited until he had sobered up to tell him what had happened. When he heard what had occurred, he "turned as if to stone"—a stroke, probably—and died ten days later.

David, a superlative warrior, could have wiped out Nabal and the rest of his household. Vengeance would have been so easy. And so wrong.

Yes, but a story from 3000 years ago does little to soothe the tortured feelings of Anne and Joe. Does God do that sort of thing today?

Of course. When God says, "Vengeance is mine!" He says it for all time. Some years ago a publishing house, on the flimsiest of evidence, summarily (and illegally!) canceled a certain writer's contracts. It had heard certain things about the writer, and it was afraid that if the facts became known, they would be detrimental to the publishing house.

Like Joe and Anne, the writer was devastated by the gross unfairness, not to mention the illegality, of the move. The writer could have taken vengeance by dragging the publishing house into the courts; the law was all on the writer's side. Litigation would have cost the company thousands of dollars in legal fees. But the writer, a Christian, did not take legal action.

Two years later, the writer bought a new car with contract advances from other houses, opportunities that had suddenly and unexpectedly opened up.

The original publishing house went into receivership.

God Understands Our Feelings When We Are Wronged.

Your Counselor knows all about being wronged! Herod tried to kill Him when He was just an infant. His disciples abandoned Him when He needed them most. One of His disciples, Peter, denied ever knowing Him. The crowd that could have influenced Pilate to let Him go chose the murderer, Barabbas, to be released instead, and the Roman guards ". . . struck Him on the head with a reed and spat on Him" (Mark 15:19). The Roman leaders allowed Him to be crucified when He had done nothing wrong. Christ received more than just a taste of human injustice; human injustice flavored His whole life and ultimately killed Him.

Yet, how in the world do you receive that kind of treatment and find a way to say "Father, forgive them . . ." (Luke 23:34) like Christ did? I can't pretend to know all the answers to that question, but I think part of the answer lies in Christ going on to say ". . . for they do not know what they do." Let me explain.

Christ understood, in the deepest possible way, that people's actions reflect who *they* are. When people spat on Him, abandoned Him, beat Him, lied about Him, mocked Him, tortured, and ultimately killed Him, Christ understood that they were revealing their own moral bankruptcy and lack of character. Another way to say it is this: Christ didn't take what they did to Him personally. That is part of what made Him Christ—He understood that what people do to us while we are here is a reflection of the doer, not the receiver.

We humans, on the other hand, take almost everything personally. I believe it is our nature to personalize what happens to us. I believe we begin life, thinking we are the center of the universe. It is our self-centered thinking, "egocentrism," the ingrained belief that everything is personal, that is often the cause of our emotional wounds and spiritual problems.

Our tendency to take everything personally is one of the main reasons we find it so difficult to forgive others when they wrong us. Simply put, we can't be truly loving and forgiving toward others when we assume that their actions are attacking the "I" within us. That is why Satan so likes us to relate to everything egocentrically.

Christ was able to say "Father, forgive them, for they do not know what they do," because He knew that what they did to Him was a reflection of them, not Him. Those who treated Him so horribly were in darkness about the truth. When people act out of their own darkness, their actions will often be destructive. Yet, we, on the receiving end of their actions, can know that it isn't truly personal. Knowing that frees us to forgive.

Now all this goes much deeper than merely understanding that people's hurtful actions aren't personal. We need to realize that we ourselves have done the same thing. In other words, whatever wrong has been done to us, we have done something similar, to someone else.

That is the message behind the story in Matthew 18:21–35 about the unmerciful servant. You may remember the story. A servant owes his master a lot of money. He can't pay and is brought to his master to talk over the problem. The master decides to throw him, his wife, and his children into prison and have all his possessions sold to repay the debt. The servant falls on his knees and begs for forgiveness, offering to pay back everything he owes over time. Sounds like how a lot of us interact with the various charge card companies. Anyway, the master takes pity on his servant and cancels his debt (I can safely say that charge card companies hardly ever do that). Remember, the servant owed a lot of money, so the master was being extremely generous and forgiving to cancel the debt.

This servant goes on his way and happens to come across a fellow servant who owes him a small amount of money. He grabs him, demanding that this fellow servant pay up. The fellow servant begs for forgiveness but receives none. The servant whose huge debt was forgiven has the servant who owed him but a small sum thrown into prison. The master who forgave the original debt hears about this and calls his servant in. He angrily gives him a tongue-lashing and tosses the merciless debtor into prison until his debt, once forgiven, is paid in full.

If we are really willing to pay attention to what this story is all about, it nails us between the eyes on the issue of being unforgiving. This story is trying to get us to realize that all of us have done horrible wrongs to others, and not to be mindful of this and forgive others for the wrongs they have done us is arrogant. Christ could honestly say that each of us owes Him all we have for the wrongs we have done, and for which He died. How can we not forgive others for the wrongs they have done us?

Selfishly, we humans want forgiveness to be a one-way street where we get off the hook for wrongs we've done, but where we don't have to let others off the hook for what they have done to us. Our sins put Christ on the cross. He died because we sinned. If we truly understand that, it would be impossible to turn around and act hatefully toward someone who has wronged us. If we could grasp that we all fall short of the glory of God, and that our sins cost Christ His life, we would be so much more forgiving of the wrongs that others have done to us.

Please don't interpret what I am saying to mean that being angry and hurt about people doing wrong to us is inappropriate, or that we are supposed to tolerate the evil done to us. There is a righteous anger and we are supposed to feel it toward evil. Jesus demonstrated it with the moneychangers. Hurt, as well, is a God-given emotion, and we are created to experience it when wronged by others. And, certainly, we need to stop people from doing wrong to us when we can. The challenge, though, is not to take things personally, and to remember that we have done the same thing to others in our own way.

Anne and Joe. What would Christ say to them? First, since we were created to experience anger and hurt, He would validate those emotions related to what happened. He would support them as they feel these feelings and grieve the situation. Second, I believe Christ would try to help them see that what happened was a reflection of the person who did the wrong, not a reflection of them. If they can see that the event wasn't personal, it would free them up to forgive. Finally, and most importantly, Christ would lovingly remind them that what was done to them is not unlike what they themselves do, either deliberately or unwittingly, and that their own wrongdoings are what put Him on the cross.

I do not believe He would be saying those things to shame them. He would tell them it is the perspective they need in order to progress from arrogant unforgiveness to humble forgiveness.

We all have been wronged, and we will be wronged again. We all have done wrong to others, and we will do wrong to others again. God has graciously forgiven our huge debt. It is time to pass that forgiveness along to others. Forgiving others is an essential element of living a healthy, Christlike life.

Have you let people who have wronged you off the hook?

VII

Don't Fit In

"And do not be conformed to this world, . . ."   Romans 12:2

Once upon a time there was a duck. She was a very proper duck who took great pride in displaying the correct plumage, in swimming smoothly, in being elegant. She brooded her clutch of eggs as all proper ducks do, and one fine spring morning they hatched. Ah, what lovely ducklings she had!

. . . All but one. The duckling that emerged from the unusually large egg was the wrong color. Its beak was so big it prevented his whole face from being cute. She would have drowned him, but he was a superb swimmer. So all summer, to her great embarrassment (and the mirth of the other barnyard fowl), this stupid, ugly, gawky kid followed her and her precious proper ducklings around the pond.

You know the rest of the story. The ugly duckling developed into a beautiful, graceful swan. Hans Christian Andersen's endearing tale has given hope to millions of ungainly preadolsecent kids the world over. Ah, to outgrow the pimple stage and become a swan!

The tale maintains its appeal because one of the most natural human desires is the desire to be accepted, not eventually, when we may possibly become swans, but right now. Ungainly, ugly, or not, we want to fit in *now*.

FITTING IN

In order to achieve that acceptance, we often do a lot of strange things, and we are not above sacrificing some of our important values and ethics. For example, I remember wanting to fit in so badly in college that I tried drinking. Personally, I couldn't stand alcoholic beverages, but I gave them a try in order to show my friends I was cool, and to gain their approval. It seemed to me that their approval was more important than my preferences.

Recently when I asked a counseling group, "Have you ever done things for no other reason than to fit in and be accepted?" and "How far did you go?" I really got a strong response. Reticent at first, the group members soon began to cut loose. Fitting in is a bell that rings for everyone.

- "I bought clothes. It didn't matter that I didn't have the money for it. I ran with a wealthy crowd and I was desperate to keep up."

- "That's how I first got involved with drugs. Unlike Bill Clinton, I inhaled."

- "How far did I go? All the way. When I was fourteen. That's how you proved you were grown up and regular. And if you were *really* sophisticated, you slept with more than one guy. I'm sure it's the guys who thought that one up."

- "Hey. There's an in crowd that's so in they don't admit they're in. Tax cheats. I'm one. I shave here, I shave there, because I figure everyone else is doing it. That's acceptance as much as greed."

These people were not convicted criminals, or sick in the head, or suffering from some weird sort of conformity addiction. All of us, to some degree, have sacrificed our morals in order to fit in and gain the world's approval.

FITTING OUT

Ask your Counselor about fitting in and He'll give you an earful. In the nonconformity department He led the way. At the age of twelve He sat in the temple even after He knew His parents were on the road home, debating theological issues with scholars—and capably, too. Throughout adulthood He went His Father's way and kept His Father's counsel. Much of the world hated Him and the claims He made for Himself and for His Father. He rendered unto Caesar and He rendered unto God, and ever and anon He knew the difference between them.

So what would He say as you sprawl, relaxed now, in His office? Christ would counsel you that if you really want to be emotionally and spiritually healthy and mature, you need to make sure you do *not* fit in. Fitting in means becoming part of a world system that is sick, and the more you become like that system, the sicker you become.

The deepest reason, the foundational cause, for the world's sickness—the original germ, if you will—is that people worship the created rather than the Creator. Think how we put people and things on pedestals and act as if they were God, rather than put God on the pedestal and give Him the honor He deserves.

Recently I saw a television commercial advertising a Michael Jackson concert. In promoting the concert, it showed clips of the fans' reactions to Michael Jackson during his show. They were swooning, fainting, screaming, and flopping all over the place. Most people would agree Michael Jackson is talented, and he has done some positive things to help people in need, but is he worth all that? What a sad commentary on our world that hundreds of thousands of young people can go into a frenzy over Michael Jackson in the contrived, artificial presentation of a concert, yet they fail to give Christ the time of day.

Your Counselor isn't surprised. He saw it coming. "I have come in

My Father's name, and you do not receive Me; if another comes in his own name, him you will receive" (John 5:43). Can you hear the frustration and sadness in His voice? He has everything to offer us, and we treat Him like an illegitimate child at a family reunion, while we adore those who have relatively little to offer us.

While that is the foundational problem, the sickness presents itself in a variety of ways. So cloaked in respectability are some of those ways, they can sneak up on you and take over your life unawares.

The arena of the workplace epitomizes the shallow, self-destructive direction that the world touts as good. I have counseled a number of men and women who sold their soul to their company in order to receive more money, a higher position, and greater status. These people have acquiesced in the company's selfish desire to promote success, but in doing so they have paid a price from which they may never recover.

One such case involved a man in his early twenties who was an accountant for a Fortune 500 firm in Dallas. He was bright, talented, and motivated, and you can bet his company was glad to take advantage of those qualities. He rarely got home before eight o'clock each night, yet he trudged back to his office at six or seven o'clock every morning. It was not unusual for him to work every Saturday and Sunday as well.

"I put in about seventy-five hours a week," he boasted. "What do I get back? Plenty! Nice bonuses, pats on the back—from some of the honchos, too—more responsibility and the pay raises to go with it. A lot of the guys I went to school with are still struggling to pay off their college loans. How many my age are pulling down the salary I do?"

Great perqs lead to bliss, right? First, he became depressed. Then he started drinking to make himself feel better. Many of his closest friendships started to die. He used to enjoy exercise; he allowed that to lapse. His spiritual life, once vibrant, melted away to nonexistence. By the time he came to see me, he looked like death warmed over and was entertaining the idea of killing himself.

For him, counseling was a means to figure out a way he could continue to work as hard as ever and still shoehorn all the things he truly enjoyed back into his life.

He wasn't too pleased when I told him that wasn't possible. And so, together, we worked on the you-can't-have-your-cake-and-eat-it-too principle, something we all learn as children and then ignore when we grow up. We explored how it is physically impossible to squeeze fourteen hours of work into a twenty-four-hour day and still have a healthy life.

Then we got down to the nitty-gritty. I showed him how, by fitting in at the company, he had given up the physical, emotional, and spiritual health that he once enjoyed. Push had now come to shove, and he was being forced by his symptoms to decide how to get his life reoriented. "Your body," I explained, "is telling you things you dare not ignore any longer. You've proven to the world how well you can fit in. Now, for your own sake, you're going to have to fit out."

I wish it were a success story. It's not. He chose not to change. His need for money, power, and praise was so strong that he refused to let them go and return to health. He was addicted, plain and simple, and could not bring himself to back off.

I know what that struggle is all about, because I have battled it myself. Success is not limited to the business world. I tried my own version of fitting in professionally, gratifying my insecurities and other people's needs in the process. I played the game pretty well, getting some of the same ego boosts that my former client did. I know for a fact that these boosts are addictive. They do feel good at the time. But just like drugs, they wear off, and you end up needing larger and larger doses of money, attention, and power to get your professional buzz. The buzz ultimately robs your life of what really matters.

WHAT THE WORLD SAYS TO YOU

We sometimes forget that the world is so lost that it glories in what ought to shame it. What is your personal arena where you yearn to fit in? What business, trade, or profession? Housekeeping? Public service? The better you fit the world's definition of success in that arena, the more the world will reward you—on its own sick terms, of course.

With what do you personally measure success? Money? Recognition? Position? Possessions? Physical strength and prowess? Cleanliness? I know a lady who cleans her entire house three times a week, top to bottom. She lives alone; she doesn't even have a cat or dog (pets are dirty). She is certain if someone drops by and sees a fleck of lint on her refrigerator she'll be considered a flop as a housekeeper.

Is that lady happy? Was the young man who sought my counsel content? Was I, when I pursued public acclaim so avidly? There is not a thing wrong with success when it is achieved for the right reasons. But success on the world's terms *always* means failure somewhere else in life when the success itself is the goal. I know. I failed miserably elsewhere, even as I succeeded in my profession. It was a painful lesson, one I hope and pray I will never repeat.

CHOOSING THE FIT

The little girl, perhaps ten years old, was taken to visit her Aunt Anne. Now Aunt Anne was, well, quite ample, and a jolly sort who loved children. "And dear," she asked enthusiastically, "what do you want to be when you grow up?"

Without hesitating, the girl replied, "A size five."

In another widely circulated little tale, a small boy was purchasing a slip for his mom for Mother's Day. Mom had mentioned she needed a slip.

"What size?" asked the clerk.

That stymied him. "Well, uh . . ." He grinned. "She's beautiful and just perfect! Does that help?"

So the sales clerk wrapped up a size ten. A few days after Mother's Day, mom brought it in and exchanged it for a size sixteen.

When it comes to size and shape, you cannot always choose exactly what you wish. Nature makes certain external demands. But when it comes to conforming to the world, you can make very clear choices. Like shoes or girdles, the wrong fit will offer nothing but pain and problems. The trick is getting the right fit—of hitching your wagon to the best star.

If true maturity and health are not tied to fitting in with the world's version of life, liberty, and the pursuit of happiness, how specifically do you go about choosing a different fit? Christ would challenge you to consider what the world dictates, and to seriously question it.

As with so many other areas of living, choosing where and how to fit in involves getting to know God's will. First may I suggest that you get out your concordance and look up *world*. An exhaustive concordance will offer you a good three columns of references. Most of them you can recite from memory once the concordance phrase has prompted you.

- John 1:10   He was in the world . . . and the world did not know Him.
- John 14:27   Not as the world gives do I give to you.
- John 18:36   If My kingdom were of this world . . .
- 1 Corinthians 1:20 God made foolish the wisdom of this world.

These examples will give you a clear picture of what your Counselor thinks about fitting into the world's standards.

Second, examine carefully what you are buying into. *Caveat emptor.* Let the buyer beware.

1. Exactly what is it that the world is trying to sell you here?

What will it cost? What benefits does it offer? Unlike the boy buying his mom's gift, you can judge with a more mature discernment. "Well, she's beautiful, but frankly, she's a little large."

In the case of the young accountant, the benefits were obvious, and he was willing to pay the price. Through therapy he gained insight into what his choices were doing to him and he made them anyway. God leaves us free to do that, you know.

In my case, I finally figured out that the long-term price did not justify the immediate benefits. That sort of insight doesn't come instantly; you must seek it.

2. Are you doing this for yourself, for God, or for the world?

It is very, very easy to rationalize an answer that suits you better than the truth. When you've decided, examine your decision again. Are you being honest?

An acquaintance of mine, sixty-two years old, bought a 1970 MGB roadster. The car was badly in need of work, but it ran. Usually. In jest, a friend accused her of entering her second childhood.

She laughed. "That I am! I always wanted a sports car someday. This is my someday."

"Now people can admire you as you tool around in that little thing."

"This pile of junk? I paid fifteen hundred for it at a garage sale." She was still smiling. "No. If no one in the whole world ever saw me driving it, I wouldn't care. This isn't for the world. This is for me. A dream realized; fun; I'm having a ball, and the world can go take a running jump."

"Oh. Then you're doing this for God."

She frowned, confused. "What does God want with a sports car with two teeth missing from the ring gear? The body's rusting out and the windshield wipers don't wipe. It's certainly upped my prayer life as I try to get where I have to go. He's probably getting tired of my constant, 'Please, God, keep it running another few miles.' But for God specifically? No."

Now there was a lady who knew exactly what she was doing, and why.

3. What will be the costs and benefits to you farther down the road?

Here are the comments of a woman who does psychiatric evaluations at a major state prison. A gentle, older lady, she has developed a solid reputation inside the walls as someone who is tough and fair.

Listen to her describe the young men and women entering prison today: "For them, there is no tomorrow. When they decide they want something, they want it now. They can't think past their noses. They can't consider consequences. It never occurs to them to think, 'If I do this now, such-and-such is going to happen to me an hour from now, or tomorrow, or next year.' They just do it—theft, rape, murder. Then they're surprised when they end up in the prison."

Our whole society—the world—is geared to the goal of immediate satisfaction. But you, as you weigh the world's claims, must look beyond the immediate, because the action you take now determines your life tomorrow. It's true, not just in that psychiatrist's prison milieu, but in every spiritual, emotional, and physical circumstance as well.

A BETTER CALLING

What is your Counselor's counsel, then, regarding fitting in? He wants you to fully understand that the world really doesn't know what it is talking about when it tells you how you should be, what you should like, what you should do; its advice will cost you.

He would have you know, too, that God offers a unique calling that requires us to fit into a different system. It means saying "No" to the things that look good but really aren't. It means saying "Yes" to God in a way that will cost you popularity and the esteem of others.

It's not all that difficult a choice, actually. The world wants you to join its club and value what it values. God wants you to join His club and value what He values. When we worship the created, we settle for temporary pleasure, if that. It will quickly turn into dregs. When we worship the Creator, we receive an abundant life. Dregs or abundance? Not really much of a choice when you think about it.

It's kind of like looking at the difference between worshiping Michael Jackson and worshiping Christ. With one, you get a two-hour, "feel good" concert. With the other, you get an eternal, "be fulfilled" life.

Been fitting in lately?

VIII

Stop Playing the Blame Game

*"So then each of us shall give account of himself to
God."* Romans 14:12

A noted politician once said, "If I could choose the state treasurer,
I'd set all the candidates down at a Monopoly game and hire the
winner." A good, rousing, cutthroat game of Monopoly brings out
the best and worst in the players, and quickly shows who is savvy,
who is ruthless, and who is too soft to survive.

Games are so popular that most large cities have stores that sell
nothing but games. Thousands of years ago, Egyptians played
board games and rolled dice. So did Celts in Ireland and the Romans. Millions of people watch "Wheel of Fortune" and "Jeopardy"
each evening. How often have you found yourself yelling at the
player on the TV screen, "Buy a vowel!"?

But the most frequently played game in the world isn't chess,
checkers, or cards. It isn't Trivial Pursuit, Pictionary, or even Monopoly. Politicians are absolutely the best players, but any person can
do it well every day.

It's called the Blame Game.

- It's my teacher's fault I got a C. She didn't explain it right.
- It's that other driver's fault; I signaled the turn.
- It's all my fault; if I weren't so clumsy, he wouldn't have gotten
  mad when I bumped him.

- It's society's fault.
- I can't help it. My parents raised me badly.

PICK THE CULPRIT

Just so that anyone can play, no matter what the attitude or hang-up, there are three variations on the Blame Game.

1. "It's All Their Fault!"

In this version of the game, the rules require that you never take personal responsibility for your emotions, your actions, or the things that go through your mind. You blame everything on outside forces that show up in your life at some time or other. Everything you think, feel, and do is caused by other people, places, or things.

This is the specialty of Calvin in the "Calvin and Hobbes" cartoon. Calvin has honed blame to a fine edge, blaming his parents; his alter ego, the stuffed tiger; Susy, his classmate; his teacher; and alien Zoworgs from space for anything that goes wrong in his life. Plenty goes wrong, too, thanks to his finely honed misanthropy.

How about you? Some guy with a beard that would dull a lawn mower blade cuts in front of you at the grocery checkout line. You blame him for the anger that erupts inside you. Your spouse throws a plate at you, so you throw a saucer back and say, "I wouldn't have thrown the saucer at you if you hadn't thrown the plate at me."

2. "It's All My Fault."

If Version One doesn't suit your reticent personality, this version of the game is sure to please you. Here, you must take full responsibility for everything that others think, feel, and do. Don't assume others are responsible for their own actions. You are no longer the victim of others' ineptness or malice. You are the victimizer. If it weren't for you, everyone would be happy.

You get caught in traffic and show up for an important meeting fifteen minutes late. The boss blows up. Obviously, you are responsible for that anger. Had you left home fifteen minutes earlier . . .

You miscount and bring too many items to the express lane in the grocery store. The guy behind you, who has only a six-pack, gets furious and makes a cutting remark. According to the rules, you take full responsibility for making him say what he did. After all, if you had counted more closely . . .

You grew up in a severely dysfunctional home. Your mom spent ten years abusing tranquilizers, your dad is an alcoholic, and your brother is doing time for armed robbery. No matter. Your poor sense of worth and trouble trusting people are all your fault.

3. "I Can't Make Up My Mind Whom to Blame, so I'll Blame All of Us."

This is a tricky version, not to be attempted by amateurs. You play it by bouncing back and forth between blaming others for what you think, feel, and do, and blaming yourself for what others think, feel and do. You are both victim and victimizer. Now you really have to be on your toes when deciding whom to blame for what. Because there is no logic to it, you can get confused and depressed easily.

At work you stumble over a wastebasket. It's someone else's fault! That wastebasket should have been placed under the desk. Your co-worker laughs at you and claims you're just clumsy. You are instantly furious with him. It's his fault you're mad; he shouldn't have said you were clumsy. You don't try to be clumsy. It's the genes you got from your bumbling father.

You head for home at the close of day. A woman coming down the street toward you is looking over her shoulder as she walks, paying no attention. She slams into you. You apologize profusely. If you had been more alert, it never would have happened. Your clumsiness has already been established; this is just one more example of it. As you turn onto your residential side street, the car behind you back-ends you. In the ensuing blame-casting, you take full responsibility. Sure your turn signal was on, but you slowed down too much. You could have turned more smartly and avoided the whole dastardly episode.

Home at last. Your castle. As you open the front door, the dog slips past you and runs out across the yard chasing a squirrel because you weren't watching sufficiently to head her off. Your daughter would have done better on her social studies test if only you had worked with her more. It's your spouse's fault dinner isn't ready.

You see now how difficult Version Three can be. Not even the dog is called to personal accountability.

Most people play one version or another of the Blame Game. Some folks specialize and become quite good at playing just one version of the game. Others do pretty well playing all the versions. If it were an actual board game that one could purchase, it would probably outsell all others. On the other hand, it's already so common, maybe no one would bother to buy it.

THE PROBLEM WITH THE GAME

The game does have its little faults. It will make your life miserable. It will keep you from growing up. It will separate you from God. Other than that. . . .

Misery? Plenty! There are truly no winners in the Blame Game. Everyone loses something. Lay blame upon others and you diminish them. Accept blame that is not yours and you inhibit their growth. As you play, your interpersonal relationships are damaged. The more troubled your relationships become, the bigger the truckload of depression, bitterness, hurt, and resentment becomes.

If you are playing Version One, blaming everyone and everything for your way of responding to life, you are being what we counselors call character disordered. Character disordered people avoid taking responsibility because they want to avoid the pain of facing their own problems. They like to make others responsible for their problems because it means that others now have to do the painful work of solving the problem.

An example: A man we'll call Jerry displayed classic character-disordered behavior. His wife nagged relentlessly. She was destroying the marriage with her incessant fault-finding and honey-do projects. If he mowed the lawn, she found fault with the work—too short, too long, not trimmed well. If he fixed the back screen door, she complained he paid too much for the new wire. It was always something. He simply could not please her. If only she would change her ways, and thank him for a job well done, he could be happy again.

You see? All the hard work has to be done by her if the marriage is to be improved.

If you are playing Version Two, where you blame yourself for everything that others think, feel, or do, you are being "neurotic." Neurotic people accept too much responsibility and tend to drain themselves. They often suffer a great deal of emotional misery as they attempt to carry the responsibility of the world on their shoulders. It is a weight that is too heavy for human shoulders, but that doesn't stop them from trying to carry it anyway.

If Jerry were neurotic instead of character disordered, he would see the problems of his marriage as being all his fault. He would rationalize that his wife was justified in expecting a better job than he was doing. If he could just get his act together, the marriage would be perfectly fine. He, you see, is taking on all the work and assuming his wife need do nothing.

Most of us are "balanced," part neurotic and part character disordered. In my own life, I too frequently see signs of both. There are times when I feel responsible for things that I really am not responsible for. For example, when I counsel, I sometimes feel that whether or not my clients improve is solely my responsibility. I find myself going home at night, hoping and praying that they will improve and feeling it will be all my fault if they don't.

The truth is that the responsibility for getting better is that client's, not mine, but I am fully responsible for my efforts to help. Ethics and Jesus Himself both require that I offer the client my very best knowledge and intuitions, bringing all my skills to play in every case. But my end responsibility is to offer insight and point the way. I cannot make the client follow that way, or even accept my guidance. Whether or not the client uses what I offer is strictly the client's responsibility. Therefore healing is within the client's perview, not mine.

On the other hand, there are times when I find myself failing to take enough responsibility. For example, I'm a great one for taking umbrage at others' insensitivity or callousness. If someone is rude, before I can think about it, I feel hurt. I see it as their fault that I am upset. Surely it's not a choice I made to feel upset by another's thoughtlessness. "If they hadn't done or said that, I wouldn't be feeling hurt like this!" It's my character-disordered mindset butting in.

While most of us are both neurotic and character disordered, usually we are more of one than of the other. Whichever trait we more frequently exhibit in life, both are a failure to take proper responsibility. Until we honestly look at which version of the Blame Game we are playing, and start taking responsibility where we need to, our lives will continue to be miserable.

There is an important growth factor we will miss, too. Maturity—that is, being grown up—involves personal accountability. The mature person accepts responsibility, and that requires diligent practice and constant examination. You don't learn to play soccer well, either, if you don't practice a lot and pay attention to what you're doing.

Maturing also involves getting past the denial stage. You're familiar with that old bugabear, denial. In fact, you can't play the Blame Game without it. You can't play Version One without denying your personal responsibility, and you can't play Version Two without denying everyone else's. It certainly does hurt to admit it when we take either too much or too little responsibility. Yet, overcoming our denial is an important starting point for the mature life God wants us to have.

THE COUNSELOR'S GAME

If you want to learn about responsibility read Matthew 23. Listen carefully to Jesus' diatribe against the religious elite. He accuses, certainly. He points to sin, yes. He condemns attitudes. But never does He take responsibility for other people's choices. Jesus, you see, being a model of full maturity, does not play the game.

We are up on a "responsibility tightrope" each day, trying to keep our balance between the two extremes of neurotic and character-disordered living. Christ wants to be the balance pole we hold on to so we don't fall off.

He never fell off His tightrope when it came to taking appropriate responsibility. As you read the Gospels, you will notice that He never blamed others for His actions. He didn't say things like, "You guys make me furious," or "You guys made me go to the cross and die." He took complete responsibility for all of His feelings and actions, knowing that He, like we, would be held accountable to God the Father for His actions.

At the same time, Christ never let other people blame Him for their problems. When they were angry or upset toward Him, He didn't moan and blame himself. Here is the Son of God who cared for all people, healing, dispelling demons, but never once slipping into the pattern of a neurotic rescuer who felt compelled to smooth over everyone's feelings.

Although Christ never assumed responsibility for what others did or how they felt, He didn't ignore their needs. He taught us that taking appropriate responsibility, letting others be responsible for their own lives, does not mean being indifferent toward them. Being responsible, as Christ defined it with His life, means being loving. Love is the most responsible act of all.

Your Counselor, then, wants to help you have an abundant life. How we handle the issue of taking responsibility will help dictate how abundant our lives will be. Will our relationships be spoiled by blaming others for our "stuff" or allowing others to blame us? Or will they enrich us? Will we begin to believe the blame we so carelessly throw about and thereby become disillusioned with life?

Christ would say, "Neither a neurotic nor a character-disordered person be!"

Are you playing the Blame Game?

IX

Don't Worry

"Be anxious for nothing, but in everything by prayer and supplication, with thanksgiving, let your requests be made known to God; and the peace of God, which surpasses all understanding, will guard your hearts and minds through Christ Jesus." Philippians 4:6–7

A number of years ago, there was a very popular song entitled, "Don't Worry, Be Happy" by Bobby McFerrin. The first time I heard it I was driving in heavy traffic in Dallas, Texas, and it couldn't have come on the radio at a better time. I laughed as the lyrics were sung, because they were so appropriate for me at that moment. I was caught up in all the hundreds of worries that seemed to be plaguing my life, wondering how I was going to handle them. The song's simple theme was that no matter how bad things get, don't worry about it—choose to be happy.

I wish it were that simple. I have always found it hard not to worry. Small things, large things, anything in my life seemed an easy launching pad for worry. When I was in high school, I worried about pimples on my face, finding a girlfriend, and making money for college. In college, I worried about passing my classes, finding a girlfriend (a constant concern), and finding a job after graduation. After graduation, I worried about finding a wife (there it is, again), getting an advanced degree, and establishing a career as a psychologist. After those issues were settled, I worried about being a good husband and father (and still do). On top all that, throughout all those years I worried about my relationship with God. Was He going to chastise me for my wrongdoings? Were He and I ever going to be close? Was I really going to end up in heaven someday?

Worry. Isn't it an awful thing? How consumed we are by it each day. It is, as Smiley Blanton once put it, "the great modern plague." We worry about important things, like making ends meet financially, keeping our marriages healthy, and raising our children properly. We also worry about relatively unimportant things, like our appearance, whether or not the lines at the grocery store will be long when we get there, and whether the soufflé we are making for the dinner party that night will rise properly. We worry a great deal in life, and we are often anything but happy because of it.

As Christ continues His work with you in counseling, He wants to let you know that if you are a Christian you don't need to worry. Unlike Bobby McFerrin, who could only encourage you not to worry, Christ can tell you why you don't need to worry. Christ wants you to know that you don't need to worry about anything because everything truly important in your life has already been taken care of for you and that you are under His protection.

Sound too simplistic? Let's look more closely.

WHAT? ME WORRY ABOUT ENEMIES?

Christ defeated the biggest enemy you have, Satan. That took place two thousand years ago when Christ lived a sinless life, died, and came back to life. To use an analogy, Satan challenged Christ at tennis and Christ beat him 6–0, 6–0, 6–0. Not only did Satan lose every game against Christ, he didn't even win a single point. No human being had ever done that against Satan before, and no human being has ever done it since. Christ came out of heaven, took human form, and did it.

Now, here is the really staggering part. Christ's flawless victory over Satan was credited to you. To use the tennis analogy, when you became a Christian Christ went to the tournament director, God the Father, and gave you credit for His victory. God erased your scores against Satan and wrote Christ's scores down by your name.

Why is that so crucial? It is crucial because God, as a perfectly righteous God, couldn't let you into heaven if you had any sin. Back to our analogy, God couldn't let you into His Tennis Hall of Fame unless you had played perfect tennis. The 6–0, 6–0, 6–0 score is the score you have to have for God to allow you to enter heaven. If you had turned in your own score against Satan, heaven could not have been yours. Christ played your match for you because you would have never won by relying on your own abilities.

If you are anything like me, this is all pretty hard to accept. First, I don't like anyone playing my matches for me. I'm one of those controllers who wants to do everything for himself. No one is going to swing the racquet on my behalf if I have anything to say about it.

Second, I don't want to admit that I can't beat my opponent. My pride has an extremely hard time admitting someone is better at something than I am. Third, I sure don't want to accept credit for something I didn't do, even if it is positive credit. I don't want to be blamed for anyone else's mistakes, and I don't want to be given credit for someone else's successes. Finally, I don't want to spend the rest of my life feeling as though I owe anybody anything for something they did for me. I don't want to be indebted to anyone.

So, everything inside my nature stiff-arms this notion that Christ played Satan on my behalf, crushed him, and then gave me credit for the match. And, even though it produces so much unnecessary worry in my life, my natural bent is to step out on the court each day and face life and Satan using my own strengths and abilities. In the process of trying to be a self-sufficient Lone Ranger, though, my worry level increases because I am overmatched. I am a novice player compared to Satan. It's no contest.

When we are overmatched, yet unwilling to admit it and get some help, worry is going to become a chronic part of our lives. Worry is a normal reaction to being in over our heads. Against Satan, we are definitely in over our heads. Why wouldn't we worry about that? It is a worrisome thing.

Yet, God no longer sees our sin, He sees His Son's blood.

Make sure you understand the implications of Christ's counseling efforts with you regarding worry in life. He is saying you can be worry-free and have every reason to be so. Worry doesn't have to be part of your life at all, because your real enemy, Satan, has been defeated. Even though you still face him each day, he has been whipped and really doesn't have the power to beat you anymore unless you let him. Only you can beat you, and that occurs when you try to live under your own power rather than let Christ live through you.

Christ is trying to tell you that when it comes to where you are going to spend eternity, you have already won because you are in Christ, and He won, and He is in heaven. If you are a Christian, you are in Heaven right now because that is where Christ is.

The issue of living life day-by-day seems like a different matter, but it is not. You can win there too by allowing Christ to live through you, and by using His power to help you overcome anything that is causing destruction in your life. Christ, in His benevolence, is offering us a winning life through His life. It is an incredible offer, better than Ginzu steak knives and the Vegamatic from Ronco.

Non-Christians are living a Lose/Lose life whether they know it or not. By not committing their life to Christ, they are going to spend eternity separated from God, in hell. That is where they lose first. Also, by not being in Christ, they lose because they do not have access to supernatural power to help them face Satan and overcome his daily attacks. Non-Christians do everything through personal power, and personal power isn't enough to defeat Satan or solve life's deepest problems.

Yet, sadly, Christians often settle for a Win/Lose life. By committing their lives to Christ, they win in the sense that they are going to spend eternity in heaven with God. That is the most important way to win in life. Unfortunately, though, many of us fail to allow Christ to live in us through the Holy Spirit while we are here, and we lose in the sense that we are often depressed, worried, bitter, unloving, and immature during our lives. Satan knows he has been defeated on the eternity issue with Christians, so his only alternative is to try to wreck the years that God gives us to live here on earth. Most of us, myself included, help him out more often than we would care to admit.

Not only has God taken care of your biggest need, salvation, through His Son, but He has also promised to help you with smaller needs each day. The classic "birds of the air" passage (see Matthew 6:25–34) is God's way of telling us that there is no need for worry concerning our basic daily needs. Let me tell you a little story to drive the point home.

WHAT? ME WORRY ABOUT THE LITTLE THINGS?

Once upon a time, there were two maids, Kunzi and Gretel. Kunzi worked for a very wealthy burgher who lived on the edge of town. Gretel worked for a mild-mannered little pensioner who possessed a tiny cottage across the road from the burgher's manor. One day a crier came riding down the highway announcing that the duke would be coming by.

"Oh dear!" cried Kunzi. "What if he stops to sup with my master?" She ran to the chicken coop, dispatched three fat hens and put them to the fire outside the kitchen door to roast. "Oh, dear! What if he should be thirsty?" And she ran to the cellar for a bucket of fine ale. "Oh, dear! What if he should tarry the night?" And she hastily prepared the tower bedchamber with a fire on the hearth and fine, clean linens.

When Gretel across the road heard the crier, she hastened to her master, who sat on his bench by the doorway of his simple cottage. "Master, what if the duke should wish to eat here?"

"God and the duke both know we've nothing but black bread. If that is not sufficient, God will provide better."

"But what if he's thirsty?"

"We've fresh, clear spring water. If that is not sufficient, God will provide."

"What if he wishes to spend the night here?"

"With the burgher's fine mansion right across the road? I doubt it. But if it be so, he may take my bed. You might set a vase of flowers on the bedstand, just in case."

Gretel could smell the birds roasting across the way, but she put away envious thoughts and contented herself with making the finest, tastiest black bread she could manage. She drew fresh water, sparkling crisp and cool, and picked a lovely bouquet of squill and wild roses for the bedside, just in case.

She looked about the cottage, smelled the aroma of roses and freshly baked bread rich in the air, and thanked God for His bounty. Let the duke come!

Now the burgher heard that the duke liked dogs, so he brought out his best hunting hound. The hound was not particularly obedient, but it looked splendid. Then the burgher, with Kunzi standing nervously behind him, waited and waited. He fidgeted. He frowned. He fretted. He rather sneered at the simple pensioner across the way, sitting there so calmly.

By and by, the duke came down the road on his splendid charger. The hound leaped up, barking, and began to worry the horse. The burgher could just picture his own head rolling if the harried horse pitched its duke into the ditch. Flustered to distraction, the burgher seized the dog and dragged it into the house. The dog squirmed free and ran for the tower bedchamber to hide.

Meanwhile, the duke dismounted to calm his horse.

"You're welcome to sit and sup with us," the pensioner called.

"Ah, good man. The burgher seems too busy to invite me. Of course I'll sup with you." The duke tied his horse nearby and joined the pensioner. Gretel hurried in to fetch the sweet black bread.

Meanwhile, the burgher cornered his dog in the chamber. But the dog backed too close to the hearth and his tail caught fire. Howling, he ran down the stairs and out of the door.

Kunzi, afraid the dog was making for the duke's roast chickens, hastily snatched them away. But they were very hot and very greasy. They popped out of her arms and into the air.

Gretel was about to apologize for the limited menu when three fine roasted birds plopped into the dust beside her, none the worse for wear. She rinsed them off with the clear spring water. She set the bucket aside and served the birds, pretty as you please. Of course, she took care to acknowledge, quite truthfully, that they were a gift of God.

The burgher snatched up the first thing he saw, the bucket of ale, to put out the dog's fire before the stupid mutt set the whole county ablaze. He tossed the ale toward the dog as they ran out into the road. He missed the dog, but instead half-filled the empty water bucket by the pensioner's door with ale.

The startled duke, the startled pensioner, and his startled maid watched the excitement briefly. Then they returned to their delicious meal of roast chicken, sweet black bread, and ale, all provided one way or another by a loving God.

WORRY VERSUS CONCERN

If you are relying on personal power to manage all the important matters in your life, you, like Kunzi, will chronically worry because you are overmatched and you are going to fail. If you are relying on God's power to help you with them, you, like Gretel, will be appropriately concerned, but will be able to focus on facing your problems, knowing that they can be successfully handled because God is up to the task.

Worry means you are tapping into yourself for the power to handle your life. Concern means you are tapping into the ultimate power source, God. Worry means you care more about yourself than the issue you are facing. Concern means you genuinely care about the issue and the people involved in it more than yourself. Worry means your pride won't let you let go of the reigns. Concern means you have let go of the reigns, but are doing all you can to help.

When we come face to face with the many difficulties inherent in life, Christ would say, "I have beaten your worst foe, and I have given you credit for the victory. Don't worry, yet be concerned. Each day presents problems that need your attention, and daily victory hangs in the balance. I will live My life through you to help you have daily victory. Since you already have eternal victory, you win twice if you give Me the reins of your life day-by-day."

Bobby McFerrin, step aside. Christ has a new song. It's called, "Don't Worry, I Won." The main stanza in the song is John 16:33: "These things I have spoken to you, that in Me you may have peace. In the world you will have tribulation; but be of good cheer, I have overcome the world." So, there is no real need to worry. All the truly threatening things about life were taken care of on the cross at Calvary, and they continue to be taken care of in the daily ministry of Christ through the Holy Spirit. We can relax in that.

Done any worrying lately?

X

Get Real

"Confess your trespasses to one another, and pray for one another, that you may be healed."　James 5:16

My kids are a lot of fun. I enjoy teasing them, and occasionally I'll say something to them that I know isn't true. For instance, I once told them that if they set off our home security system, the place would immediately blow up. Another time, I told them that they couldn't get married until they were thirty-seven or God would take them home to heaven early. Okay; I admit that wasn't the best, but believe me, they're onto me. With the wrinkled nose and supercilious tone only a kid can muster, they come right back with, "Yeah, sure, Dad. Get real."

"Get real." Pretty good advice, actually. A lot of us go through life rarely getting real. We frequently walk with a mask on, taking it off maybe once or twice a lifetime to let others see who lives behind it. I have already mentioned that we often wear masks to earn people's approval and protect ourselves from emotional injury, but whatever the motivation, our masks often stay on and we remain unknown. The less known we are, the less healthy we are. That is why Satan likes us to wear masks. We never get real, and we never mature.

FALSE FACES

Bill, a man in California, worked for a while as the night guard on a movie set. "What an eye-opener!" And indeed his eyes grew wide just talking about it. "It was a western, and the building that looked on the outside like a bank was actually the property warehouse. Dozens of guns, and not a one that actually shot bullets. The coffee pots didn't hold coffee, the woodstove wouldn't burn wood, and the food was plastic.

"Anyway, this one night I stepped inside and swept it with my flashlight, like I always did. And right in the flashlight beam, up on a carton, a rattlesnake was coiled. All I could think was, 'If that buzzer gets down in all this stored junk, we'll never dig him out!' I figured I had one shot to take him out. If I missed, he'd be over the side and hiding who knows where. He didn't move as I got closer. And closer. And closer. He was rubber! I guess a rattlesnake figured in the story somehow. Man, that rattler looked absolutely real. Took ten years off my life, right there, and added three dozen grey hairs."

Make believe. You don't really believe all those bullets in the gangster movies are real, do you? You don't really believe true love works out the way the romance novelists suggest. Compare the storyline of the recent "Last of the Mohicans" film with James Fenimore Cooper's original novel. They're worlds apart, and yet they're both make-believe.

But the entertainment industry has no monopoly on make believe. Every one of us plays the game daily, wearing masks of expedience or fear.

There are a variety of masks to serve every occasion.

- The "I'm fine" mask covers up the fact that we aren't doing so well.
- The "I don't need anyone" mask covers up how lonely we are.
- The "Let me help you" mask keeps other people from helping us.
- The "I'm angry" mask actually hides the sadness we feel.
- The "I'm helpless" mask conceals our fears about growing up, about taking on mature responsibility.
- The "I'm better than you" mask cleverly disguises how inferior we feel.

Hide your internal struggle; pick a mask. Hypocrisy comes in many guises.

Make believe your life is in order or someone might find out it's not.

Because ours is such a mask-wearing society—another sign of the world's sickness—few dare to take their masks off. Others might ridicule or judge them when they do. Remember when Senator Thomas Eagleton was selected to be Senator Eugene McCarthy's running mate in the 1972 presidential campaign? He took off his mask and admitted to having been treated for depression in a mental hospital. He had to drop off the ticket because public reaction was so negative. So much for honesty in the public domain. People who tell the truth find it used against them. No wonder they quickly put their masks back on, never to take them off again.

Where can you find some of the most flagrant cases of mask-wearing? Sorry; it's churches. The very place supposedly characterized by people being real with one another is often the last place where being real actually occurs. Critics from outside (and occasionally from within) claim the church is full of hypocrites. Sure it is. So is the world outside the church, because hypocrisy comes so naturally to human beings and, until Christ returns and sets things right, the church is full of fallible human beings. Still, that's no justification. *People in the church should be free of masks. People in the church should be honest.*

What are some of the pretty masks you see, and what are some of the ugly truths behind them?

- I attend church faithfully. (Of course, I sleep through the sermon.)
- I am an upstanding citizen. (The fact that I cheat my employer, routinely exceed the speed limit, and fudge at solitaire is beside the point.)
- Sexual misadventure is shocking! (But it sure is fun.)
- I am happy and well-adjusted, with a smile for everyone (and ready to cut my own throat—or my spouse's).

- I love everybody! (I can't stand interacting with them.)
- I follow Jesus (when there's nothing better to do and/or it suits my purposes)!
- [Divorce] [Gossip] [Sexual perversion] [Abuse] is sin (except when I do it; then it's only a justifiable mistake)!

I'll bet you can add a dozen of your own. Sadly, unless the masks come off, the local church cannot be the place of healing that it is supposed to be.

UGLY FACE

An eight-year-old was asked whether it was ever okay to lie.

"Sure," was his instant reply.

"Oh." All those Sunday school lectures had obviously fallen on deaf ears. "When is it okay to lie?"

"Birthdays."

He has a point. In his home, what the gift is is never revealed until the recipient opens it. Often, the family members go to elaborate lengths to maintain the happy secret. Also, his mom had just sprung a super surprise birthday party on his dad. So maybe there is a place for masks. "Gee, I don't know what you're getting for your birthday." (And you're going to love it!)

Birthdays aside, masks and make believe do three unhealthy things.

They hide the true us so others cannot help us or support us.

When the deli clerk asks, "How are you today?" she does not expect an account of your last three doctor visits. A "fine, thank you. And how are you?" suffices in that superficial moment. But when your pastor, or doctor, or best friend asks the question, and means it, it behooves you to remove your mask. You need the pastor's prayer, the doctor's professional care, the friend's support and compassion.

They hide us from ourselves.

As long as we convince ourselves that all is well, we don't have to do anything to improve matters. And yet, unless we grow and improve, we are doomed to unhappiness and ineffectualness. We cannot stay babies and serve God well. We cannot stay babies and love well. We cannot develop strong friendships or solid marriages without admitting problems and then setting out to solve them.

They hide the truth about the life of faith.

How often have you gained the impression from some church that everything is just wonderful in it? No problems, no worries, no sins. "We just give it all over to Jesus and stay happy all the day." The outsider looks at the false face of this church and makes one of two assumptions: Either it is full of goody-goodies and the outsider would never be able to fit, or the outfit is lying through its teeth and the outsider doesn't want to be a part of it. Neither assumption serves Christ, who came into this world to save sinners.

A realistic and honest self-evaluation—that is, without masks—is the only course a strong instrument of Christ dare take. Nothing less will serve His purposes. Jesus Christ's church has never been perfect. The original apostles fell short in many areas. So do we. To paint a make believe picture that everything is always hunky-dory destroys the very integrity we are supposed to have as Christians.

Masks in the church reap misery far beyond the local body. When Jim and Tammy Bakker fell from grace, religious charities across the board felt the repercussions when donations dropped drastically. Financial malfeasance in one organization, carefully hidden, and then exposed traumatically by persons outside the church, unfairly painted all ministries with the same brush.

TRUE FACE

In the light of all this, Christ has another piece of counseling He wants us to hear: take your mask off and get real.

As He hung on the cross, He cried out, "My God! My God! Why have You forsaken me?" (Mark 15:34). It was, in a sense, a rhetorical question. His rational mind knew the answer. He had to suffer like this and die to pay for the world's sins. He knew that all along. But in agony, rational thinking is the first thing to disappear. When His whole universe had narrowed down to three spikes and two boards, He let His emotions show for all to see. Never in His life had He worn a mask, and He wore none now. He was forsaken by God Himself, His own Father, and He freely admitted it in the most poignant and heart-rending cry the world has ever heard.

Again, as always, your Counselor led the way. What you saw was what you got. He took great pains to say exactly what He thought and felt and meant. He didn't pretty it up just to make everyone feel better about Him. He was straightforward with His disciples about his pain and problems in life. He didn't act strong when He felt un-happy or sad. He was the real thing and stayed that way the whole time He was alive. He provides, in the matter of masks as with every other matter, the mark toward which we ought to strive. All His cards were on the table, whether you liked His cards or not.

"No way!" you say. "That was He. This is me. Do you know how far Jesus would get if he were walking the earth today? A bearded guy, never straying beyond his little patch of the Near East? Thanks, but no thanks. I'll keep my mask on. I feel safer behind it."

I know. I often feel the same way. Why should I take my mask off if nobody else will do the same? I fear being different. Even more, I fear being exposed. Why risk exposing myself to ridicule and rejec-tion by those who are too immature to handle what I reveal about myself?

Yet, before you bolt your mask down and weld it on permanently, stop and think about it for a minute. What price have you paid for the mask you wear? They don't come free, you know.

Has wearing it brought you closer to people, or has it made all your relationships shallow and distant? With the surface tightly cov-ered, who can get beneath it?

Are you teaching your kids how to build healthy, interpersonal relationships, or are you teaching them how to create masks? Are they getting an accurate picture of how to function in adulthood?

Has wearing it helped you mature as a person, or has it kept you from developing?

Have you really helped others with your mask on, or have you offered a lot of insincere advice that didn't really make a difference?

If you are truly honest about the price you have paid for wearing your various masks, you will have to admit that the cost has been astronomically high. The mask has to come off or you will continue to pay dearly in the form of shallow relationships, inner loneliness, emotional turmoil, and spiritual emptiness. Besides, your kids are learning from you every minute of the day. Do you want to watch them pay the same high price?

I speak from experience. My own masks have been many, and the cost of wearing them looks like the national debt. I have worn nearly all the ones I mentioned above. They served the purpose of keeping people from seeing my pain and insecurities, but they also kept me from being close to people and, worst of all, close to God.

One of my masks, strangely enough, has been the mask of psychologist. I can see now that I have hidden behind that mask for many years. It is a variation of the "Let me help you" mask. I wear it to say "I'm here to help you," when underneath is a troubled soul that really wants and needs help for itself.

It isn't hypocrisy as such, nor is the problem painted in black and white. I genuinely care about people and earnestly want to help them. But the psychologist mask allows me to play the role of the wise, authoritative counselor while at the same time enabling me to run from all the things in my own soul that are a mess. It allows me to examine the plank in other people's eyes while totally ignoring the one in my own.

I wonder if a lot of my colleagues aren't the same way. Maybe I am projecting my own experiences onto them, but I sense that most of my peers in the counseling field are troubled folks in their own right and are running from their own problems by hiding behind the mask of psychiatrist, psychologist, therapist, or counselor. We often hear that psychiatrists have the highest suicide rate among professionals, and I wonder if that doesn't support what I am talking about. Rare are the counselors who are earnestly working on their own issues as they attempt to help others do the same. Most of us don't mind putting others under the counseling microscope; we sure don't like going under it ourselves.

In my own efforts to battle this problem of not getting real—of hiding behind the masks in my life—I once organized a Get Real group with four of my trusted friends. All counselors, we met once a month for dinner and then spent the rest of the evening (about three hours) getting pretty transparent with each other. It was painful, but it was helpful. We each opened up areas of our lives that we were struggling with, and which we felt embarrassed about. There were more than a few tears shed.

The safety of that group allowed us the confidence of knowing that we were accepted and supported regardless of what we shared. The group became one place in our lives where we could quit playing games and tell it like it was. The Get Real Gang disbanded when three of us moved, but all of us will look back on that time as one of the most important periods in which we were able to mature.

Recently, I helped to start another Get Real group with colleagues here in Austin. I am looking forward to seeing how God will use it to help me—and us—be more like His Son.

How do you go about ripping your mask off? Simply stated, direct your efforts toward becoming more transparent. Let specifically chosen people know who you are and what you are struggling with. Don't keep everything bottled inside. Let it out so you can get some help with it. Don't lie. Risk that frightening transparency, even if some people reject you because of it.

Let me offer a word of caution, though, about taking the mask off and letting people see what is underneath. Maybe it goes without saying, but good judgment needs to be employed when deciding with whom to be frank and what to share about yourself. Getting real is a good thing, but it is inappropriate to confide in casual acquaintances. You want to be transparent with those closest to you, but even then good judgment is required.

So, in His efforts to counsel you, Christ would lovingly challenge you to get real, as He is. Let some trustworthy, God-respecting people see who you are so they can help you. Wearing your mask only makes you sicker, and people will often get sick of the mask you wear. Ultimately, you don't fool anyone. Believe me: Eventually most people will see right through you. "You can fool some of the people all of the time, and all of the people some of the time, but you can't fool all of the people all of the time"—words as wise today as when first they were spoken.

There are people out there who would like you to take your mask off so they can be close to you and help you. They can't do either if you play games with them.

God would put His name first on the list of those who would like to see you take your mask off, for your sake. There is nothing true about you that He doesn't already know. Nothing you are or have done has escaped His notice, and He still loves you and is deeply committed to helping you. I know you have heard that before, until, maybe, you are sick to death of it. Yet it is God with whom we most need to be honest. Ultimately, He cares more than anyone else about our struggles. Take your mask off with Him—He already sees behind it.

Your friends, your family, God Himself are all waiting.

Is your mask still on?

XI

Solve the Paradoxes

*"I say to you, unless a grain of wheat falls into the ground
and dies, it remains alone; but if it dies, it produces much
grain."* John 12:24

Riddle: A father and his son go for an automobile ride. They are
involved in an accident, and the father is killed. The child, badly
injured, is whisked off to the hospital for surgery. The doctor comes
in, takes one look at the lad and says, "I cannot operate on this boy,
because he is my son." How can this be?

This story involves what seems to be a clear contradiction. How is
it possible that the boy is the doctor's son when the boy's father just
died? The solution to the apparent contradiction, of course, is that
the doctor is the boy's mother. A child with a female pediatrician
would not see a problem in the first place. But those of us who were
raised with the cultural mindset that doctors are men often find ourselves unable to see the obvious. In not being able to see the obvious, our minds scramble around for other explanations that often
take us in ludicrous directions.

"Well, uh, maybe it has to do with a secret paternity thing; baby
swapping, you know?"

"The doctor failed to correctly identify the kid."

"The driver of the car was a priest; you know, Father Murphy or
something, with his spiritual son."

Life seems full of paradoxes and conundrums. A paradox is a dual statement that seems to contradict itself and yet expresses an element of truth. A conundrum is a riddle or a question apparently without an answer. Paradoxes and such can be extremely frustrating to grapple with because they appear to be so clearly contradictory. And yet, learning to understand them can open up new views about reality that can change our lives.

The Bible offers us some important paradoxes to explore. The healthy Christian life is very much tied to tuning in on God's frequency, and His frequency is often tied to paradoxes that are hard to grasp but crucial to understand if our lives are to be full and complete. Our Counselor wants each of us to face these paradoxes, because by doing so we will end up with a deeper, more meaningful life experience. After all, He is the one who planted them.

To Live You Must Die

Everyone knows what an amoeba is, sort of, but have you ever really seen one? They're microscopic water creatures. You knew that. And they can change shape. You also knew that. Stained, fixed and somewhat squashed under a glass slide, they look mostly like blobs. Alive, they're fascinating.

Amoebae are three-dimensional blobs in real life, able to change shape from spheres to ovals, without pseudopods or clubby extensions sticking out. Lacking mouthparts or anything of that sort, they eat by engulfing. They bump into a food particle and simply continue around it. Where the amoeba makes contact with itself on the far side of the particle, its membrane dissolves and its "body," so to speak, fuses. The food particle is now captured within the three-dimensional amoeba. There, digestive enzymes and other chemical tricks will turn it into energy and amoeba building-and-repair substances.

Most of the time, the amoeba reproduces by dividing. The nucleus replicates itself into two identical nuclei. The amoeba's "body" divides down the middle, sort of a reverse of its engulfing technique, and donates about half of its body substance to each nucleus. Each half-sized amoeba then captures food with which to grow.

From one, two. But this division into genetically identical twins cannot go on indefinitely. The daughter cells lose the ability to reach full size. The amoeba's nucleic material needs rejuvenating, and that means union with nucleic material from another individual.

To accomplish genetic recombination, two amoebae meet and touch. At the point of contact their external membranes dissolve and mix together. In a sense, they engulf each other. The resultant superamoeba, with twice as much nucleic material as it needs, soon divides again, making two amoebae with the normal gene count. But the genetic material differs now. No longer are all A's cells together and all B's cells together. Instead, the nuclei carry a mix of A and B. Refreshed and rejuvenated, the two recombined amoebae will divide again and again, reproducing asexually for a number of generations until the call comes again to recombine.

So, when the two came together sexually ("sexual" is a misnomer in a way; the term "meiosis" fits better), which one died?

Both.

Neither.

The animal is still alive. *But it is not the same animal.*

Now let's pretend that there's this superintelligent amoeba, who can see what's coming if he joins another amoeba in that rejuvenating union. "I'll lose my uniqueness!" he'd cry. "I would no longer be me. To protect my one-of-a-kind self, I must avoid meiosis at all costs."

Protect the self! Save the self. Everywhere we turn, we are assured that the self is the most important thing, and that we are supposed to do everything we can to promote it. Self-esteem, self-worth, self-concept, self-fulfillment, self-enhancement, self-determination, self-promotion, and self-adoration are just some of the terms that are rampant in our society, making us the most self-absorbed nation on earth.

Christ would have none of that when He was here. Even though

He was God, He came to serve, not to be served. He died to self, figuratively, and eventually, literally. He made Himself completely available to God the Father. "Not My will but Thine." Can you imagine how hard it was to say those words then, particularly at that place and time (Gethsemane at the hour of His passion)? He was committed to service during His life on earth, and He carried through with that commitment into death.

It's no piece of cake now. Still, Christ knew, and wants us to know, that true meaning and fulfillment in life comes from serving, not being served. The Bible is very clear about that.

For our lives to have deep, lasting impact, we have to give up self-preoccupation and self-promotion for a life of service that is centered on helping others and pleasing God. As hard as it is to do, it is the only truly healthy route to go in life.

To genuinely live, we have to die. We have to die to that part in each of us that wants to be the center of the universe at everyone else's expense. Our narcissistic focus on self has to be replaced with a Christlike focus on loving others.

Unfortunately, being able to die to self is not possible through personal willpower. Selfishness is too strong a force for human effort to overcome it. That is why God has to empower our efforts. Without His help on the issue, we will continue to be dominated by self rather than consumed with Him. As we have seen throughout this book, "Unless God builds the house, we labor in vain" (see Psalm 127:1). This is especially true when it comes to dying to self.

You protest, "But I'll be like a rudderless ship. Like a horse without a bridle."

Ever ride a horse?

"Sure."

In battle?

"Uh, no."

Cavalry horses were superbly trained to respond correctly during the heat of battle. The riders had to concentrate on dealing with the enemy, not on making their horses behave. The horses obeyed what is called "the aids." These were cues other than the reins and the bit: the way the rider's weight shifted, and how the rider's knees and calves and toes pressed the horse's sides. A good horse would stop, go, and turn anywhere its master instructed, whether the rider had a hand free or not.

All that skill, all that training disappeared if a horse lost its rider. The horse would change from a confident, terrible war machine to an addled ninny the moment the cavalryman went down. It would slam about mindlessly and gallop about wildly. No hand on the reins, no weight in the saddle, no direction.

Does that sound a little like you? Your self is like a cavalry horse without a rider.

"But if I forego taking care of myself, I'm going to die."

Hardly. To truly die to self requires a deeper understanding and appreciation of how committed God is to taking care of our needs. If we can grasp that He will look out for us and meet those needs that He put in us, we can more easily let go of the reins of our life. We grasp those reins so firmly because we really don't understand that we have a loving Father who is committed to meeting our needs. True dying to self is fundamentally tied to knowing that it is God's very nature to take care of His children. If we know that about Him, then being preoccupied with our own needs seems rather foolish.

To really live, we must die. A great paradox, but one you can base your life on.

To Be Wise You Must Be Foolish

Graduate school was an interesting time for me. I remember thinking how exciting it was to study so many different issues relating to people and their problems. It was a real head trip as I, along with my fellow graduate students, grew in knowledge. I remember walking around campus feeling superior at times to those who were *mere* undergraduates.

Eleven years later, I can appreciate that I was actually an intellectual midget. What I learned that greatly impressed me back then now seems like so much foolishness. Since earning a doctoral degree, God has shown me in many different ways how the wisdom of man is truly foolishness, and how God's "foolishness" is great wisdom.

Christ saw the same problem with worldly wisdom in His day. The Pharisees were considered the intellectual and spiritual elite of the day, and they seemed proud of that fact. Their pride in what they knew was really an indication of just how foolish they were. From Christ's perspective, they were in darkness. That is why Christ told His disciples, "Let them [the Pharisees] alone. They are blind leaders of the blind. And if the blind leads the blind, both will fall into a ditch" (Matthew 15:14). The Pharisees, who were so impressive to the people of their day and so impressed with themselves, were the most foolish people of all. They were leading people into a pit, and they were too blind to know what they were doing.

I see my own education in psychology in that light. What was passed off as great wisdom during my graduate school years was often just so much psychobabble. Even though my professors were quite earnest in their desire to train us students into becoming competent psychologists, they, at times, passed along blindness in their teachings. I, not really being careful to stay grounded in the Scriptures, believed a lot of what they taught. So did my fellow students. Since then, I have had to do more unlearning than learning. I have more earnestly tried to take the advice Christ gave to His own disciples, and I have chosen to return to what Christ had to say and made that the central focus of my life and my counseling efforts.

Paul, in his letter to the church in Corinth, was greatly concerned about the very thing being discussed here. You know how some cities develop a reputation as an intellectual center? In Paul's day, Corinth was one such city. The Corinthian culture represented the accumulation of knowledge from all the known world, and the Corinthians had gladly placed their trust in this knowledge.

Yet, Paul writes these words to the Christians in Corinth: "Let no one deceive himself. If anyone among you seems to be wise in this age, let him become a fool that he may become wise. For the wisdom of this world is foolishness with God. For it is written, 'He catches the wise in their own craftiness'; and again, 'The LORD knows the thoughts of the wise, that they are futile'" (1 Corinthians 3:18–20). Paul was letting the believers in Corinth know that true wisdom is based in realizing how little the world understands and how much we need to depend on God for what we think.

Basically, when it comes right down to it, there is earthly wisdom and heavenly wisdom. Most of us settle for the former, when the latter is what really sets us free. In order to be truly wise, we have to accept the prospect of being seen as foolish in the world's eyes. I know the sting of this teaching whenever I talk with non-Christian psychologists about Christianity. They often look at me as if I have totally lost my mind.

At those moments, I have to work hard to remember what Paul told Timothy: "For the time will come when they will not endure sound doctrine, but according to their own desires, because they have itching ears, they will heap up for themselves teachers; and they will turn their ears away from the truth, and be turned aside to fables. But you be watchful in all things, endure afflictions, do the work of an evangelist, fulfill your ministry" (2 Timothy 4:3–5).

Have you fallen into a pit by listening to the world's wisdom, or have you become foolish by listening to God's wisdom. Let me encourage you to be a fool.

To Be Strong You Must Be Weak

You're probably too young to remember the Charles Atlas ads in the old comic books. They are where we get the phrase "97-pound weakling." Here's this droopy little skinny guy at the beach with a fairly neat girl. Along comes a guy built like a professional wrestler on steroids. He deliberately kicks sand in the skinny guy's face. The girl hops up and walks off into the sunset on the bully's arm. Don't let this happen to you, the ad says.

Charles Atlas sold body-building. His philosophy was the stronger you were, the less sand you would have to wash out of your eyes.

Weakness is unacceptable.

Few, if any of us, enjoy being weak. Actually, we hate it. When it comes right down to it, most of us will do anything we can to avoid appearing weak. "Be strong," "Look confident," and "Never let them see you sweat," are just a few of the things we tell ourselves and others most days. Underneath it all is the horribly mistaken notion that to acknowledge weakness is a sin.

In our culture there is such a tremendous emphasis on being strong that we have become a culture of cover-up artists who put on the makeup of "I'm strong" when the real truth underneath is "I'm weak but I'm just too afraid to admit it."

When was the last time you honestly let someone know how weak you were in a given area of your life? Was there ever such an occasion? Most of the time, weren't you trying to put your best foot forward with others so that you could impress them? The best foot forward includes eliminating any hint that you have a weakness or soft spot. Maybe, like me, you expend a lot of effort trying to appear to be something you are really not—strong!

Another great paradox in life that Christ would want us to grapple with is that it is by admitting our weaknesses we become strong. It is in acknowledging that we don't have all the intellect and power and wherewithal to be successful in the things that matter, and that the beginning point for true growth and development in life is admitting just how weak and incapable we are. Try that thought out in a culture that has bought into the baloney that personal power is the name of the game, and that you can pull your own strings to achieve a successful life if you want to.

Whenever I pull my own strings, I get tangled up in them.

Please don't hear what I am saying as an encouragement to use your personal weaknesses as an excuse for a life of laziness and self-indulgence. Not at all! Being weak is the opposite of self-indulgence. The self doesn't get nearly as much attention when efforts are centered on growth.

Admitting to weakness is critical, yet our weaknesses are no reason to throw up our hands and say "I quit" in the face of challenges that overwhelm us. We all walk a fine line here between the appropriate humility of "I can't do it," and the copping out of "Since I can't do it, I'm off the hook for any effort on my part to learn to do it."

Paul, once again, is a key person to turn to when dealing with this paradox. Having received great revelation from God, there was the potential for Paul to become conceited. So, he was given a "thorn in the flesh" that greatly tormented him. We aren't sure what that thorn was, but it was obviously quite burdensome to Paul because he pleaded with God to take it away from him.

God did not take it away from Paul but instead told him, "My grace is sufficient for you, for My strength is made perfect in weakness."

Paul learned a valuable lesson from this, and responds with these words: "Therefore most gladly I will rather boast in my infirmities, that the power of Christ may rest upon me. Therefore I take pleasure in infirmities, in reproaches, in needs, in persecutions, in distresses, for Christ's sake. For when I am weak, then I am strong" (2 Corinthians 12:9–10).

I don't pretend to fully understand this paradox, but I do know that it is God's way of telling us that in the humility of seeing that we don't have it all together He can use us greatly for His will. In a culture that says, "Don't admit your weaknesses to anyone," Christ is telling us to let people see our weaknesses and even boast of them so that Christ, Who has no weaknesses, can work through us. If it is not our strength, it is His, and He is therefore glorified.

My moments of greatest personal weakness came when I was trying to pretend I was self-sufficient and strong, and my moments of greatest personal strength were when I was able to admit to being needy and weak. Maybe that has been true for you as well. Christ wants to use those experiences to teach us to depend on Him rather than ourselves for the power to do what we do. When Paul depended on Him, the lives of thousands were changed. That can be true for us as well. We can have that kind of influence on others if we let Christ do it through us.

Are you a weak person trying to pretend you are strong, or are you a strong person because you know how weak you are?

AH, THE PARADOX OF IT ALL

Three tough paradoxes have been discussed in this chapter. Whereas the world would say, "Live, be wise, be strong," God says, "Die, be foolish, be weak." Quite a difference!

The Christian life is not just riddled with paradoxes—the Christian life itself is the ultimate paradox.

Here is how A. W. Tozer so accurately describes it: "A real Christian is an odd number anyway. He feels supreme love for one whom he has never seen. He talks familiarly every day to someone he cannot see, expects to go to heaven on the virtue of another, empties himself in order that he might be full, admits he is wrong so he can be declared right, goes down in order to get up. He is strongest when he is weakest, richest when he is poorest, and happiest when he feels worst. He dies so he can live, forsakes in order to have, gives away so he can keep, sees the invisible, hears the inaudible, and knows that which passeth knowledge."

So it is in understanding and living out these paradoxes that the Christian can have life in full. Whereas Christ used paradoxes to confound the wise of His day, for the Christian with spiritual ears to hear these paradoxes Christ points the way to overcoming the problems that plague us.

Want to overcome what you are struggling with? Die!

Be foolish!

Above all, be weak.

XII

Agape Everybody

"Love your neighbor as yourself."   Matthew 22:39

Dionysius the Elder, tyrant of Syracuse, could get away with murder. He proved it by condemning Pythias, an innocent man, to death. Pythias begged for a little time to put his affairs in order. His friend, Damon, offered to stand in his place. If Pythias failed to return on time, Damon offered to be executed instead. Dionysius acquiesced; after all, one man was neither more nor less guilty than the other.

Pythias left town to complete his affairs. When the time of execution arrived, Pythias had not returned and Damon was led away. Onlookers, not to mention Dionysius himself, marveled that Damon still believed Pythias would return. At the last moment, as the executioner's blade was about to fall, Pythias came, bursting through the crowd to take his place. He had been delayed, but now he was here.

There erupted an argument between, of all people, the two staunch friends, not unlike an argument you might hear at lunch: "Let me pay the check." "No, no, I insist. Let me." But this one was, "Let me die this unjust death in your stead." "No, no, I insist. Let me." Dionysius, flabbergasted, intervened, pardoned them both, and pleaded to be admitted into their steadfast friendship.

Such is the power of genuine love.

THE MANY FACES OF LOVE

What a curious language is English! It ranks as one of the world's most expressive languages, having a word for every purpose. For example, what would you call a bunch of trees? Orchard. Grove. Stand. Forest. Wood or woods. Thicket. Woodlot. Copse. Park (in the technical sense). No two of those words mean exactly the same thing. On the other hand, there is "fix." I can fix you a drink, fix the flat tire, get in a fix, fix a traffic ticket, fix dinner (why? Is it broken?), and fix you up on a date.

The word "love," like "fix," has become generic. I love my car. I love to travel. I love ice cream. I love my wife. I'd love to see the game today. I'm in love. . . . As if love were flexible enough to be applied to cars, travel, romance, ball games and summer treats. I love it!

The Greeks, of which Damon, Pythias, and Dionysius were three, used a suite of different words for the ambiguous English term *love.* The Greek word *eros* has to do with romantic and sexual feelings. From it comes our word *erotic.* Glorious as it can sometimes be, *eros* is, perhaps, the least demanding of the loves, interested in little more than the physical. *Phileo* has to do with friendship feelings. "Brotherly love," *phileo* is sometimes called. This is how Philadelphia, the City of Brotherly Love, got its name—*phileo,* love, and *adelphos,* brother. *Phileo* is a reciprocating love; that is, so long as you love me, I'll love you. If your love dies, mine is bound to wither.

And then there is *agape* (pronounced uh-GAH-peh). *Agape* is the love Damon and Pythias shared. It transcends *eros;* the physical shrinks to insignificance. It soars beyond *phileo,* for it is complete, not reciprocal. If your love dies, mine will remain constant. I can *agape* you whether you return my affection or not, even if you don't realize I exist.

Can one face of love turn into another? It depends. Frequently I'll hear of some unwise girl who, because she desires to marry some young man, allows him *eros,* hoping it will blossom into *agape* and they will live happily ever after. Many a movie plot illustrates that theme. Rarely, if ever, does it happen in real life.

Phileo, though, can be the natural precursor to *agape.* In the famous passage of John 21:15–17, Jesus asked Peter, "Do you love (*agape*) Me?"

Now Peter, for all his rough and ready ways, was an honest man. "You know I love (*phileo*) You."

Jesus asked again, using *agape.* Good old Peter. He knew which way the wind blew, but he couldn't bring himself to lie. "Yes, Lord, I love (*phileo*) You."

The third time, Jesus took a big step down. "Peter, do you love (*phileo*) Me?" To quote the seventeenth verse, "Peter was grieved because He said to him the third time, 'Do you love (*phileo*) Me?'" In a way, Peter was letting down Jesus, and it tore his conscience. God agaped Peter. Peter phileoed back.

Eventually, the salty old Galilean did indeed reach the high mark. We know, because years later he was able to write in his second letter, ". . . giving all diligence, add to your faith virtue, to virtue knowledge, to knowledge self-control, to self-control perseverance, to perseverance godliness, to godliness brotherly kindness (*phileo*), and to brotherly kindness (*phileo*) love (*agape*)" (2 Peter 1:5–7).

Agape is the version of love on which the Bible focuses. It is the word used in the "Love your neighbor as yourself" passage in Matthew 22:39. It appears in the other key passages, such as "For God so loved the world . . ." (John 3:16), and where Christ refers to the love that God the Father has for him in John 17:26. In fact, whenever Scripture says that God loves, *agape* is the word used. Complete, total, sacrificial, requited-or-not love.

TRUE LOVE

Mushy emotions and sexual impulses. That's the lesson we learn about true love from television and movies. We probably learn far more about love from our parents than from the TV screen. What do our parents teach?

"If you behave yourself, and obey me, I'll love you." Far too often parents attach conditions to their love, and thus teach their children that love is something you have to earn through obedience and good behavior.

By the time many of us reach adulthood, what we've learned about "true love" has become so distorted. And yet, it is critically important to understand the meaning of "love" as our Counselor of Counselors uses it, because His two greatest commandments center around it.

What would He tell you as you sit in counsel? His exact words are recorded in Mark 12:29–31, "'. . . you shall love the LORD your God with all your heart, with all your soul, with all your mind, and with all your strength.' This is the first commandment. And the second, like it, is this: 'You shall love your neighbor as yourself.' There is no other commandment greater than these" (*agape* is used throughout). How can we attempt to live our lives by these core commandments if we don't have any idea what "love" really is?

So from the way Scripture employs the concept of *agape,* and from the way Jesus Christ Himself uses it, I would define true love as "an action aimed at helping someone grow whether he deserves that help or not." What does that mean in practical terms?

First, love is action.

Love involves doing something, rather than just experiencing some warm fuzzy feeling or basking in some vague thought. To say it as Peter would say it, you have to take action if you would truly love someone.

Harry, the bus driver, says, "I love my kids. I want to spend more time with them." Talk is cheap. Voicing those sentiments is not love. Thinking them is not love. Assuming other parts of the definition are met, doing it is love. That means Harry has to sacrifice some of his own free time in order to put his love into action. Asked to fill in for another driver by taking an extra route on his day off, he might have to pass up the offer (and miss out on the overtime pay!).

Can his little kids pick up on it and appreciate it for what it is—love? You bet! They may not be able to articulate it verbally or even think it consciously, but they will learn the important lesson. Love is action.

Second, love attempts to foster growth.

When the Army urges you to "Be all that you can be," rest assured the Army does not *agape* you so completely that it helps you to excel for your own sake. The Army, quite selfishly, wants and needs people at their best. By bringing out your best, the Army serves its own needs. Fostering growth, of and by itself, is not love.

This is one important reason why *eros* is not true love. Romantic love and sexual desire hunger for another person as he or she is now, not for what that person might become. Potential has very little to do with *eros;* immediate satisfaction has everything to do with it. *Eros* does not—cannot—concern itself with the beloved's future growth and development. *Eros* is too tightly focused on now.

Harry, the bus driver, takes the time to teach his kids how to change the oil in the car, how to shoot baskets, how to balance a checkbook. And he teaches the children the most important thing of all—to love the Lord. He both models and teaches justice, responsibility, honesty and valor, not so he'll look good in their eyes, but because these are traits they have to know, and such abilities do not occur in children spontaneously. He loves them enough to do what's best for them now and in the future. A practical attribute of *agape* love is always the beloved's growth and well-being. But there is more.

Third, love is unrelated to deservedness.

Harry loves his kids. He loves his wife. He can't stand the old man next door. Why? The dolt has a dog that never stops barking. Try to enjoy a Sunday afternoon on your patio with a "Cujo" yelping to wake the dead next door. "Believe me," claims Harry, "that bozo next door doesn't deserve to be loved!"

Agape ignores the dog. *Agape* excuses the mess and noise. *Agape* wears earplugs if necessary, though earplugs if *agape* is already in place, probably won't be necessary. A tactful word to the neighbor—"I'll be getting in really late. Can you keep your dog in the house until eight tomorrow morning? I'd sure appreciate it!"— will probably be sufficient. If not, *agape* works around it. *Agape* does not wait for the neighbor, or the child, or the mate, or the parent, or the total stranger to shape up. *Agape* loves as is. Such love does not assess whether a person has been good enough to be treated lovingly. Love in its true form is aimed at all persons, no matter how wonderful or despicable they are, or how objectionable their actions may be.

ALL TOGETHER NOW . . .

For true love to occur, then, all three elements must be in place—action, a desire to foster wholesome growth, and no assessment of deservedness. We fail to be truly loving if any part of the definition is not in place.

Harry's brother, Eddie, also a bus driver, really loves his kids and wants to spend time with them, but he's too tired when he gets home to do much, and he needs those extra shifts on weekends to put food on the table. Eddie misses the mark.

Eddie wants his kids to behave well and obey the law, because you know how the courts are these days. Your kid gets in trouble and whammy! Some do-good social worker sticks you out in front of the magistrate, when it was your kid who went joy-riding. Besides, if your kid runs a little wild, what do the neighbors say? Eddie wants to be well thought of; he wants the neighbors to identify him as a good father. Eddie does not encourage his kids to respect the law for their benefit as they become adults; he's doing it to look good. No *agape* there.

Eddie is willing to spend all the time it takes to help his kid improve at basketball, but his kid has to practice hard and play hard.

Be the best on the team! But Eddie isn't about to put any time or effort into the kid if the kid doesn't care enough to *really* want to excel. Eddie just put a price on his love in action. Conditional love, it's called, but not *agape.*

Eddie would be the first to say, "Are you kidding? The kind of love you're talking about is impossible! Nobody's *that* good! Your definition is too drastic."

As hard as true love is to define, I agree, it's even harder to do. If *agape* were easy, Damon and Pythias would not have maintained their legendary fame for 2400 years. Our natural bent as human beings is to neglect to take action for someone else's betterment. Most of us find it difficult enough to extend ourselves occasionally for the betterment of those we care about, much less to do the same for people we dislike. That is why I so firmly believe that true *agape* love is a supernatural accomplishment. We must rely on God to do it through us, or it won't get done.

Ask your true Counselor about *agape.* He'll just smile. His love for us took the highest form—entering our world to die for us. You've heard many times that God sent His Only Son to die for our sins. In a way, that's unfortunate, for you've heard it so often it's become old hat. So stop. Let's pick that apart, and study it in detail. Let's look at it from a fresh perspective.

THE ULTIMATE *AGAPE*

Here is the Cocreator, the Lord of the galaxies, delivered at birth by lamplight. What a come-down. From heaven to a livestock shed. For more than thirty years, He suffered cold, wet, thirst, heat, ridicule, hatred, hunger, misinterpretation, temptations, His followers' ignorance, Peter's impetuousness and uncouth language, James and John's lack of charity, Nicodemus's cowardice, and finally, Judas's betrayal. If that's not the ultimate love in action . . . !

One of the primary reasons Jesus Christ allowed His own death on the cross was to provide us with the opportunity for a deep and intimate walk with Him. God sacrificed His Son on the cross—and Jesus, instead of fleeing, went willingly—so that we could grow spiritually into true children of God.

And do we deserve all these gifts? Have we earned them?

As Paul points out in Romans 5:6–9, "For when we were still without strength, in due time Christ died for the ungodly. For scarcely for a righteous man will one die; yet perhaps for a good man someone would even dare to die. But God demonstrates His own love (*agape*) toward us; in that while we were still sinners, Christ died for us. Much more then, having now been justified by His blood, we shall be saved from wrath through Him."

You see? He went into action to provide us an unearned advantage, thereby, as Paul points out, demonstrating what *agape* is all about. There can never be a greater example of love than what God did on the cross. This is the love felt toward you by the Counselor in whose office you now sit.

By demonstrating love, God gave us something to which we could compare our actions. Be honest now. How do your efforts, and mine, compare with God's efforts? None of us comes out looking very good.

Why would a loving God show us up so badly? He makes our efforts at love look putrid in order to humble us and to break us from the notion that we, on our own, can love others deeply. Both humility and brokenness, in turn, are designed to drive us into the arms of God for the help we must have if we are ever to be able to offer others or ourselves true love at all.

God doesn't make us earn His love. It is truly given to us with no strings attached. But He does want us to return His love, and to love others as well as ourselves. We don't *have* to respond to His love by loving in return. He wants us to *want* to love Him. See the difference? Of course, as we truly begin to grasp the depth of His love, it becomes almost impossible not to pass it along. God's love, when encountered fully, is as overwhelming as that.

AS THE TWIG IS BENT . . .

. . . So grows the tree. A friend I know watched a bonsai demonstration not long ago, at a horticultural meeting. Bonsai is the Japanese art of miniaturizing living plants, usually trees. The trees are planted in very shallow dirt, so that their root systems are limited, thus stunting their top growth. They are severely pruned and clipped.

"Isn't this a cruel way to treat a tree?" my friend asked.

The bonsai artist smiled and shook his head. "Cruel? Not at all. In the first place, there is no pain involved. Bonsai are not starved or neglected. On the contrary, they're fed well and watered often. They are extremely well cared for, but they're not pampered. They're outdoor plants receiving only a minimum of shelter. They live for hundreds of years, quite comfortably."

Then he took a length of soft copper wire and skillfully wrapped it around an interior branch of his little tree. He wound the wire round and round in a coil nearly the whole length of the stem. Then he gently, carefully, bent the branch into a new shape, sending it in a new direction. "The wire will hold the branch in its new place," he explained to the crowd. "In nine months or so the branch will have adopted its new configuration. I will remove the wire and the branch will stay as I shaped it."

The bonsai artist, in effect, was distorting his little tree so that the relatively young plant (ten or fifteen years old, he said) would look like a gnarled and twisted old patriarch of the forest, but in miniature. The artist distorted the tree on purpose. Distortions happen to us, too, accidentally, often to our detriment.

The adage, "As the twig is bent, so grows the tree," is normally applied to the rearing of children. I mentioned previously that parents can distort our perceptions of love by attaching conditions to their affection. The media and our culture can also distort our concept of love by dwelling on *eros* and the superficial at the expense of depth. As the twig is bent by all this outside influence, so goes the tree—us.

A lot of distortion occurs from the inside, too. You've heard these statements; perhaps you've even made some of them:

- "I work all those extra hours because I love my family and want to provide well for them."
- "I love my friend. That's why I don't say anything to her about what she did to me the other day."
- "I love him/her so much I can't stand to be without him/her."

Statements of love? In each case, we are imbuing ourselves with motives of love in order to cover up our selfishness. Selfishness is a great distorter! Indeed, some of the most selfish and destructive things we do are often done in the name of love. You see, if we rationalize our actions as being loving—in order to fool ourselves and others—we aren't likely to see any great need to change them. Even Judas betrayed our Counselor with a kiss.

When God challenges us to love our neighbor *as ourselves,* I believe God is telling us that not only are we to help others mature by what we do, but we are to do that which encourages our own maturity and development as well. To love ourselves the deepest way possible means, therefore, to choose to follow God's plan for our lives because His plan creates the greatest level of maturity, peace, and joy.

Christ was aware of that when He was tempted by Satan. What would you do if Satan offered you all the kingdoms of the world as he did Christ? You could bring peace to the world by stopping all the bickering and armed conflict. No more traffic tickets. Your own airplane. No one to criticize you. No more Form 1040. But Christ saw through the offer. He fully understood that Satan's route would lead to self-destruction and that God's route would lead to blessing. The most unloving thing Christ could have done that day would have been to settle for the deal Satan was offering. The most loving thing he could do was what He did—the Father's will. To do God's will under pressure is the highest form of loving ourselves.

I spent most of my Christian life thinking that God was a killjoy and that all His commandments and challenges were meant to make life miserable for me. Well—if not miserable, at least dull and boring. I realize now, after having gone my own self-destructive way more often than I care to admit, that God only asks of us those things that either bring something good into our lives or help us avoid something bad.

God is benevolent in every request He makes of us. If we can fully grasp that, as Christ did, it makes no sense to go any other route than God's. Doing His will becomes irresistible rather than inhibiting.

"Very well," you say, "explain. What specifically do I do? Don't just exhort me. Put the cookies on the bottom shelf where I can reach them."

PUTTING LOVE TO WORK

Even if we agree on how to define love, it is still difficult to know what course of action love might require us to take. Basically, what you do for someone must be evaluated on an individual basis.

Maybe a friend has innocently gotten himself into financial trouble. Flattered that some big East Coast banks were courting him, the friend took on too many financial commitments, and now the interest payments on his debt are sopping up nearly a third of his paycheck. Is it loving to give him the money to pay off some of the debt, or is it better to encourage him to find some other way out of his problem?

My son has a tough homework assignment. I don't tell him this, but I think his teacher asked altogether too much of him in this instance. Is it loving to help him do it or do I insist that he work it out on his own?

Let's say I work in a mortgage brokerage firm. The woman in the cubicle next to me is angry with our office manager. Do I listen to her and to the manager without taking sides? If one is clearly wrong, do I take sides? Do I refuse to listen or become involved until they've tried to work it out for themselves?

My best friend is about to marry and I am convinced that disaster looms. The girl he's so infatuated with (and I'm certain it's little more than infatuation) is really not good for him, and he can't see it. Am I being loving to tell him what I see, or do I respect the fact that he's an intelligent adult and it's none of my business?

Am I my brother's keeper?

What is Christlike? May I suggest you first study the Gospels, no matter how often you have read them in the past, to see what Christ did. Knowing He demonstrated perfect *agape,* analyze His actions. There were times when needy people clamored for His attention—*needy* people—but He made them wait while He went off alone to pray. As His disciples' boat was crossing a stormy sea, He did not take a hand on the lines and tiller. He fell asleep. Seek out these and other situations. Jesus Christ came to serve others, but He did not always do what they wanted Him to do for them. And He took care of Himself. He maintained His spiritual and physical strength.

Will an hour or two of TV relax me? Yes. Do I need relaxation? Sometimes. Can I serve more people if I take on extra work? Yes. Efficiently and well? Maybe not.

What, then, is the measure?

1. Does it do the object of the action good? (The object, the person I'm serving, might be someone else or it might be me.)
2. Does it prevent (further) harm?

Simple as those two guidelines sound, they require immense discernment and wisdom. We must rely on God's guidance by examining Christ's life in detail and by constant, fervent prayer.

What are the answers to the situations above? I don't know. Perhaps my son will indeed grow if pushed, and then I would do well to encourage him without actually doing his work for him. Perhaps my friend with the overextended credit has learned his lesson. If he has not, what can I do to help him avoid repeating the mistake? Discernment.

Review the questions I posed above. Pretend someone you know is in a similar situation. You see how additional information can fine-tune your own actions? What would you do? What options would you have—what differing courses of action would you take? Get yourself thinking selflessly.

SELFLESS LOVE

"Love suffers long and is kind; love does not envy; love does not parade itself, is not puffed up; does not behave rudely, does not seek its own, is not provoked, thinks no evil; does not rejoice in iniquity, but rejoices in the truth; bears all things, believes all things, hopes all things, endures all things" (1 Corinthians 13:4–7).

What an amazing description of what love is all about!

And now I propose a challenge. Choose someone with whom you are close—a spouse, a child, a coworker. Put that person's name in each of the statements in the love passage.

As an example, I would choose my wife, Holly. "I will be patient with Holly. I will be kind to Holly. I will not envy Holly. I will not boast around Holly. I will not be prideful around Holly (but I certainly am proud *of* her!). I will not be rude toward Holly. I will not be self-seeking with Holly. I will not be easily angered with Holly; I will not keep a mental tally of her wrongs. I will not delight in evil around Holly, and she and I will rejoice in truth. I will protect her, trust her, hope with her and in her. With Holly, I will persevere."

When I put the name of a loved one on that passage, I get a clearer sense of just how tough true love is. But that's not all!

"I will be patient with myself. I will be kind to myself. I will not hurt myself by envying, boasting, being proud. I won't be rude to myself, or self-seeking; neither will I injure myself by being easily angered, and *I will not keep a record of my personal wrongs* (oh, how many times in counsel I see patients who simply cannot forgive themselves of some error!). I will not injure myself by delighting in evil but will help myself by delighting in truth. I will allow God in His love to protect me; I will trust in Him, hope in Him, persevere for Him."

Can you imagine what your life would be like if you offered others and yourself this kind of love? Christ not only wants you to imagine it, but to do it. Love is not just a nice idea. It's a command from God Himself. It is an essential requirement your Counselor would put before you. If you refuse or neglect (they end up being the same thing) to love others and yourself, you are refusing to overcome your problems.

Have you *agaped* anyone lately?

XIII

Never Quit!

"And let us not grow weary while doing good, for in due season we shall reap if we do not lose heart."   Galatians 6:9

For a number of years my brothers and I would gather with our families in San Diego for a week of vacation during the summer. During our time together we would go to the beach, ride bikes, take walks, go out to eat, and spend countless hours talking about all the things that mattered to us. Those vacations were always a time of great enjoyment, something that we always looked forward to.

As part of our vacation together, my brothers and I would participate in a half-marathon that the city organized. Don't ask me why we did it, because I can't really tell you. Something about brotherhood and bonding and fresh southern Californian air. Anyway, we would get up early on race day, around 5 A.M., dress, drive to a pick-up location, catch a bus to the race site, and wait with thousands of other runners for the start of the race. All of that (except for getting up at 5 A.M.!) was the fun part.

Once the race began, it became a little bit less fun. A half-marathon is a distance of 13.1 miles. Let me say that again—13.1 miles. That we would get up at 5 A.M. to run 13.1 miles should tell you that my brothers and I don't have a lot of common sense. Now, I don't jog for exercise (racquetball is my way of staying in shape), so running one mile, much less thirteen of them, wasn't something my body was prepared for each summer.

It didn't take but the first few miles of the race for me to discover I was in the wrong place at the wrong time doing the wrong thing. My legs would hurt, my lungs would feel as though they were on fire, and my back would ache. And you can bet I let my brothers know about it. I whined like a banshee to get them back for convincing me to do such a stupid thing. I guess I figured that if I made things miserable enough for them during the race, they would quit wanting me to run it with them each year.

Seven or eight miles into the race, it was even worse. My body was yelling at me, "Chris, you idiot! Stop this nonsense immediately. You are going to die if you don't cease and desist." But, I guess I just couldn't have lived with myself if I had let my brothers finish the race without me, so I kept going.

The people who put on the race must be sadists, because the very end of the course is a semi-steep section of street leading into Balboa Park. Now, make sure you heard that. We have run about twelve miles, and our reward for all that blood, sweat and tears is that we get to run uphill to the finish line. I am glad people can't read my mind at that point, concerning what I think of the organizers of the race.

The last three hundred yards, though, are worth it all. The course levels off as it enters Balboa Park, and it is one beautiful place. Vivid green lawns and lovely plantings frame the various public buildings. The tall gum trees, both gangling and stately, line the borders and pleasant walkways.

And the whole stretch is lined with people cheering you on to the finish line. I always get chills on that last stretch, and the fact that my body is about to die no longer seems to matter. My brothers and I run the race side by side, so that we finish at the same time. One of my most prized possessions is a picture my sister-in-law, Donna, took of the three of us as we neared the finish line one year. After we cross the finish line, our wives take more pictures of us as we tell them what a piece of cake the race was (we are a bunch of liars). You get to act supremely macho at that point.

After we have had our pictures taken and have lied sufficiently, we join all the other runners in an area of the park where the refreshments, rub downs, and race shirts are. It is always gratifying after having finished a difficult run to be around all the other runners. We all know how tough the race has been, and there is a sense of shared accomplishment that goes unspoken. Besides, no one knows how fast you ran the race, so you can act as if you crossed the line with the first twenty-five, or even broke the course record, and no one knows any better.

The T-shirt given each runner was a memento that said you were foolish enough to run the race. For months and years afterwards, until it was too tattered to keep, I would wear my half-marathon T-shirt with a great sense of pride. The fact that the first place finisher completed the course in half the time it took my brothers and me is something I would not mention to others who asked me about the shirt. My policy was that what they didn't know couldn't hurt them.

Now, I am telling you this to make a point about something else Christ would work on with you if He were your counselor. Christ knows that the race called life is long and painful. He knows that we grow weary in life and often want to quit. The challenges of being married (or single), raising children, doing quality work on the job, developing deep friendships, keeping up with day-to-day demands, and, most importantly, trying to be close to God are, when taken all together, a heavy load. That heavy load makes life quite a challenge.

Christ knows all this, having gone through a tough time here on earth Himself, and He knows how tempting it is to say, "Forget it! I'm quitting." Yet, He would encourage all of us to never give ourselves the option of quitting in our efforts to reach the finish line. No matter how much it hurts or how badly we want to stop, we are to press on to the very end. As always, He set the perfect example. When your emotions hurt, and your mind is on fire, and your soul aches, finishing the race of life is easier said than done and is a real test of one's courage.

The motivation for running the half-marathon becomes pretty murky about two miles into the race, at least for me. Just whom am I trying to please here? Whom am I trying to impress? For Christians, the biggest source of motivation to run the race of life is to please God. If we truly understand what it meant for Him to come down from heaven, become one of us, and die for our sins, we will want to run to please Him. God gave His all for us, and, if we can fully grasp that, we will want to give our all back to Him as a way of thanking Him for His efforts on our behalf.

While running the race of life, God will use various people to encourage us along the way. Running with my brothers was like that. We would support each other throughout the race, keeping each other up as best we could. If one of us stumbled, the others would be there to help him get back on his feet. Also, it was helpful when people along the race course would shout encouragement, like "Keep it up! You're doing great! You can make it!" Those statements made a world of difference during the race. The Bible has numerous "one another" verses that emphasize how important a role we all play in helping each other make it through life. We need to allow others to encourage us toward the finish line, and we need to do the same for them.

Another invaluable way that God helps us while we are on the racecourse of life is through His word. While on the course, we need a clear mind in order to handle the challenges of the race. For my part, I like to dream up dastardly ways to get even with the turkeys who dreamed up that final uphill leg.

Even better, God's Word provides us with all the truth we need to know about anything we may encounter during life. It is a tremendous source of encouragement and comfort, and He wants us constantly to meditate on it while facing life. Psalm 119:105 says, "Your word is a lamp to my feet/And a light to my path." When on the racecourse of life, you don't want to run in darkness, and God's

Word keeps you from doing that. The race is a lot easier when you can see where you are going.

Another critical issue is: what is the motivation for finishing the race? What if that final hill were steeper? What if the second or third leg of the race were so difficult my knees threatened to give out? I could reason: there's no use crippling yourself for life for the sake of getting a T-shirt. Why bother to finish? Run until it doesn't feel good anymore and then quit.

Finishing the race of life has to do with what is waiting for us at the finish line. In the half-marathon I really looked forward to reaching the beauty of Balboa Park, being able to rest, getting some refreshment, being with the other runners, and getting to wear the T-shirt that signified I had completed the race. The parallel in life is that heaven is waiting for us when we finish. Heaven makes Balboa Park look like a cesspool. Heaven is our true home, and we run the race here looking forward to being there. There, there will be no suffering. There, everyone will truly love each other. There, our lives will be complete in every way. And, most importantly, there, we get to be with God and enjoy Him forever. What fantastic refreshments are waiting for us at the end of our lives here, refreshments that genuinely and eternally refresh! It is really something to be excited about and to motivate us to run the race of life with greater commitment and effort.

A significant difference, though, between literally running a race and running the race of Christianity is that in the race to be like Christ you don't ever cross the finish line while you are alive. True Christlikeness is something we are always in pursuit of, but it is never something we attain while in these human bodies. So, while my brothers and I always finished the half-marathon, we, as Christians, can only keep diligently moving in the direction of the finish line of being like Christ, knowing that we will never get there until we get to heaven.

Before we leave that thought, though, there is something very important about the fact that we can never be just like Christ while here on earth. The goal of being like Christ brings more out of us than if we had settled for a less challenging task. In the half-marathon, because the race course was 13.1 miles, we ran 13.1 miles. If we had entered a one-mile run, we would have only run one mile. The point is this: What you set your sights on tends to dictate how far you actually go. The goal of being like Christ, which is always out of reach, challenges us so that we end up being much more loving and mature during our lives than we would have been if we had modeled our lives on someone else.

It is because we are constantly in pursuit of being like Christ that Paul, the premier Christian of his day, said what has to be the theme of every Christian's life: "Brethren, I do not count myself to have apprehended; but one thing I do, forgetting those things which are behind and reaching forward to those things which are ahead, I press toward the goal for the prize of the upward call of God in Christ Jesus" (Philippians 3:13–14). We will never take hold of perfection until we take hold of heaven. Until we get to heaven, life is a constant straining to win the prize of being just like Christ and of being with God forever.

So, while the race of life is painful, we run with great enthusiasm and dedication because we want to please God for all He has done for us. While running, He will use other Christians, the truths of His Word, and the awesomeness of heaven to motivate us. Our goal in the race is to be more and more like Christ each day. While we never are exactly like Christ while here, we aren't discouraged by that fact because all God asks is that we keep moving in His direction. However far short we fall of being like Christ, having Him as our "mark" helps us become much more complete human beings than if we had settled for a lesser life than Christ's to be our model.

I have at long last come to my senses—I no longer run that half-marathon every summer. I think advancing age, a busier life, and a modicum of brains have won out over that particular version of enjoying brotherhood, bonding, and fresh, southern Californian air. Yet, each of us, just like you, are still running together each year in a much more important race—the race to be like Christ. My brothers and I, as brothers in the Lord, are excited about running the race to be like Christ, and then we are looking forward to bonding completely in heaven as we worship God in perfect harmony forever. Until we get to heaven, with God's help, we will never quit trying to be like Christ.

In your own life, many times you may feel like quitting. The problems you face may seem so overwhelming that there may appear to be no alternative except to give up. Please allow me to encourage you that the God you serve is bigger than any problem you face, and that He will help you overcome those things that weigh you down. God wants you to keep striving to be like His Son no matter how hopeless things may seem at times. With God as your running partner, no race in life is too long or too difficult. Stick with God and He will ultimately take you to your real home in heaven where you won't have to run anymore.

The race to Balboa Park, in the scheme of things, was a frivolous pursuit, and the reward—a T-shirt. The race we run daily for Christ is the opposite of frivolous, every step counts, and the reward—eternity with God.

When it comes to growing closer to God and being more like His Son, never, ever, for any reason whatsoever, quit.

XIV

What Christ Wouldn't Tell You If He Were Your Counselor

"Beware lest anyone cheat you through philosophy and empty deceit, according to the tradition of men, according to the basic principles of the world, and not according to Christ." Colossians 2:8

A television channel—in fact, a whole network—devoted to shopping. Thousands of mail-order catalogues offering everything from computers and dinosaur-shaped muffin pans to automobile parts and lawn tractors. Malls with ice rinks; you come to skate, you stay to buy. Wow! These modern sales pitches!

But an elderly neighbor merely smiled at all the opportunities to spend money these days. She was sitting on the swing on her front porch one pleasant autumn evening simply talking. That in itself is almost a lost art; few houses other than hers have a spacious front porch, and among those that do have a porch, few have a lovely varnished swing hanging on its chains from the porch ceiling.

"You're too young and too urban to remember the traveling shows," she said to a thirty-seven-year-old friend. "I grew up in a village in rural Ohio. This was right after the war—the late forties. A show came to town, rented the school auditorium, and entertained us for five nights straight. Fifty years ago, and I still remember the baggy-pants clown. Padukey was his name."

"A vaudeville type show?"

"That's right. There was no television then, and there were no theaters anywhere near. No city-type entertainments. We flocked to watch the stupidest acts, and loved them. Then during every show there were the sales pitches for liniment and salves."

"Snake oil."

"Snake oil. Cheaply made cures that didn't work, for outlandish prices—especially aimed at farmers back in those days. A dollar a bottle? My mother's salary was twenty-five dollars a week working at the bank. And, of course, there was popcorn and Cracker Jack for sale." She waved a hand. "So you see, each day and age has its hard-sell experts. Sure, there's more available to buy nowadays. But fifty years ago, in our own way, we were getting the high-pressure sales pitches, too."

Her friend thought about that for a moment. She nodded. "I see. And the products they hawked were specifically chosen to appeal to a particular audience—farmers and small town people, who needed medicines and had no ready access to them."

"Give them what they think they need to improve their well-being. As true then as it is now." The older lady smiled sadly. "And I doubt the quality of the goods has improved at all."

It certainly is true today. People these days have an abundance of material things. Most of us eat well (some of us too well). So, people tend to focus on their mental and emotional well-being. And there are a multitude of seminar speakers, authors, and counselors ready to help them do just that.

SELF-HELP NON-HELP

I must confess that I feel a fair amount of embarrassment when I walk into a bookstore and look at the different titles in the psychology/self-help section. I am amazed at the incredible amount of misguided trash that is being offered to the public by people in my profession. It isn't that these books don't have some valid points in them, because most of them do. It's just that most of these books point readers in the wrong direction. Sadly, even some Christian self-help books fall into the same trap.

I'm convinced a lot of these books ought to have warning labels on them that say, "Caution! The material in this book is potentially harmful to your mental and spiritual health!" When it comes to a lot of popular self-help books, *caveat emptor*. Let the buyer beware!

The problem goes beyond the self-help literature, though. The field of secular counseling and some versions of Christian counseling need to come with a warning label. Thousands of therapists are engaged in counseling which, like many self-help books, has some validity, but which often goes off in directions that can be quite harmful to the client.

However, I don't say that as if I am above it all. I have made my considerable contribution to this very problem. My own lack of experience and blind spots during my professional life have resulted in my offering clients counseling that didn't exactly hit the mark. Oh, I tried; my motives were good, but my understanding was not. Even now, I find it a tough challenge to hit that mark with each client I see.

In this chapter, I want to counter some of the ideas that are popular in many secular approaches to counseling. Why? Because I believe these precepts are ones that Christ would *not* tell you if He were your counselor. I believe He wants all of us to be cautious about what we buy into regarding personal growth, and He wants us to know that we can't trust a lot of what is being offered by the so-called self-help experts.

Christ Wouldn't Tell You "You Are O.K."

"The evil that men do lives after them. The good is oft interred with their bones." Shakespeare, in *Julius Caesar*.

"Put a teaspoon of wine in sewage, you have sewage. Put a teaspoon of sewage in wine, you have sewage."

"No good deed goes unpunished."

"The good die young."

"How to swim with the sharks . . ."

You'd think, from statements and old saws like the above, that being good simply isn't worth the price. It's the good that gets the bad press, if it gets any press at all. It's the good that fades. We'll remember Hitler longer than we'll remember Albert Schweitzer. So why is it so many counselors and self-help practitioners so desperately try to convince us that we are good at heart? What's so glamorous about being good, if all those axioms above are true?

As I discussed in Chapter Three, a lot of people in the counseling field, and many who write the best-selling self-help books, teach that we are basically good. They buy into the humanistic notion that people, by nature, are inherently kind, decent, and caring, and that with proper love and support from others, they will naturally grow into fully mature human beings.

What hogwash! People aren't basically good, they are basically selfish and self-serving! While most self-help books are trying to help elevate our sense of inherent decency and worth based on who we are, God is diligently trying to kill off that part of us and help us see that we only have worth because of who He is.

I'm not O.K. and you are not O.K., I don't care what mental health experts tell you in their popular books. Whether we want to hear it or not, we are all stained at our very core by selfishness, and that makes us anything but O.K.

Yet, we love to hear someone tell us that we are wonderful! It tickles our ears to be told that we are awesome, and we gladly give our complete attention to anyone who tells us that. John Calvin, in Institutes of the Christian Religion, put it this way:

"Accordingly, in every age, he who is most forward in extolling the excellence of human nature is received with the loudest applause. But be this heralding of human excellence what it may, by teaching man to rest in himself it does nothing more than fascinate by its sweetness and, at the same time, so delude as to drown in perdition all who assent to it. Whosoever, therefore, gives heed to those teachers who merely employ us in contemplating our good qualities, so far from making progress in self-knowledge, will be plunged into the most pernicious ignorance."

Christ would not tell us that we are O.K. because He is inherently honest, and the truth is we are inherently fallen. Our deepest motives are selfish and horribly impure. As one person put it, even our tears over personal wrongdoing have to be washed clean in the blood of Christ. Yet, at the same time, Christ would want us to know that we were made in His image and that we have worth because of that. So, as Francis Schaeffer stated so simply and eloquently, "Man is sinful and wonderful."

Don't listen to anyone who tells you you are inherently good, because you aren't. Yet, don't let anyone tell you you are trash, because God doesn't make junk. Christ wants you to see that you are both fallen and precious. One without the other falls woefully short of the truth. Depending on only half the truth will make your trip through life miserable.

Christ Wouldn't Tell You "You Can Do It"

Because you can't. So there.

Another message we often get from self-help psychology is that no matter what you must overcome, with enough insight and elbow grease you can somehow overcome it. "You can do it!" the message says.

This popular message encourages us to believe that we have enough personal power to persevere, whatever ails us, and that we can become whatever we want to be. So, not only are we told that we are inherently wonderful, but we are also told that internally we have all the resources we need for a successful life.

Again, what absolute hogwash! When it comes to saving ourselves spiritually, we certainly didn't have the power to do that.

Christ had to do it for us. And, when it comes to our day-to-day lives and how they turn out, I don't believe we have enough personal power to be truly successful on that level either. Yes, I know that others would vehemently argue with me on this issue, but I don't see anyone being a mature, Christlike human being on personal power only. It just can't be done.

The insufficiency of personal power to bring about true, deep change is why Christ has to live His life through us in order for our lives to become mature. He knows we don't have it in us to consistently think the truth, or stay on the moral path, or love people deeply, or sacrifice for the good of others. Christ can certainly do those things through us, but we can't do them on our own.

Many self-help books will tell you otherwise, though. They will tell you that you can do anything you set your mind to, that you've got it (whatever "it" is), and that you can be in control at all times. Put that to the test, though. Try to do anything you set your mind to.

- Picture two million Presidents of the United States.
- Picture two million women married to Robert Redford, or Christian Slater, or Sean Connery, or whoever the heartthrob of the moment may be.
- Picture two million men winning the Indianapolis 500.
- Picture two million little kids romping with real live mutant turtles in some city sewer.
- Picture yourself solving all your own problems and living a carefree life ever after.

I would like to be a perfectly loving human being, but believing it in my mind doesn't make it so. What vanity it is to believe we can do anything we set our mind to.

It isn't vanity, though, to believe God can do anything He wants through us. He can achieve through you what you would never be able to achieve on your own. He can help you love others who are hateful to you. He can help you learn how to sacrifice for the good of others with no strings attached. Only He can help you do these things. They are not natural accomplishments, they are supernatural accomplishments.

Trying to be a mature, loving human being using personal power is like trying to power a luxury cruise liner with two "C" batteries. You just can't get it done with such a limited, inherently deficient, power source. So, don't let anyone tell you otherwise. The bottom line is that you can't do it. Christ has to do it through you.

Christ Wouldn't Tell You "Be Happy"

The emphasis in a lot of popular self-help books and counseling is on personal happiness. "Overcome your problem by [fill in the blank] and be happy!" is the theme song of many books and counselors. Happiness is held up as the ultimate goal in life. Our founding fathers dreamt of a land that would provide us the freedom to pursue happiness if we choose, but modern Americans seem to think that the happiness itself is constitutionally guaranteed. And many advisors would try to convince us that the true happiness that is our right is readily obtainable through certain insights or techniques.

I don't believe Christ would go so far as to tell you to pursue happiness. No, I am not saying He is a killjoy and anti-happiness. I just don't believe He wants happiness to be our main focus. I believe that Christ would encourage us to pursue maturity, not happiness. And, as you well know, the pursuit of maturity sometimes involves being unhappy. To truly mature means being willing to suffer the pains of learning to love others as much as you love yourself, to give when you want to take, and to submit when you want to run the show. The reality of trying to do what it takes to mature is that you will be very unhappy at times.

I want to admit to speaking out of both sides of my mouth on this issue, though. When my first book, *The Lies We Believe*, came out, the publisher and I struggled with what statement or phrase to put on the cover. We finally put the statement "The #1 Cause of Our Unhappiness" on the cover next to the title. I always felt uncomfortable with that choice of words, because it implied that the focus was on overcoming our lies so that we could be happy. I really feel that God wants us to overcome our lies so that we can be mature and free in order to serve Him better. Happiness will be part of that process at times, but is not supposed to be the central focus of our lives.

While here on earth, we have to live with some realities that are not happy.

- We are not yet with God.
- We all have self-destructive tendencies that cause great pain to ourselves and others.
- Life here on earth is fraught with illness, trauma, financial and emotional reverses—a myriad things going wrong.

In the face of these realities, happiness isn't what we want to feel. We, like the apostle Paul, groan to be with God in heaven. Life on earth will be appropriately unhappy at times until we go to be with God.

Christ Wouldn't Tell You "Look Out for Yourself Only"

Another way, then, in which a lot of self-help books miss the mark is through overemphasizing self-protection and self-preoccupation. To hear many books tell it, you have to look out for yourself, be your own best friend, and win by intimidation if you want to be happy and successful. Many of these books foster an "every man for himself" attitude which encourages a self-absorbed, "I'll take care of myself" stance in life.

This kind of guidance ignores the reality of a loving God who has promised to meet all our needs. It also ignores how that loving God wants us to be mutually interdependent as we go through life. God created us with needs, and He is more than prepared to meet them if we will let Him. By constantly straining to meet our own needs, we push God aside. We become self-serving rather than God-serving.

I believe Christ would tell us not to worry about our own needs because God will meet them. In light of that, I believe we are to be more concerned about the needs of others than about our own. That isn't to say that being concerned about our own needs is wrong or selfish. It is to say that being preoccupied with our own needs is an indication that we are not only playing God, we are not acknowledging the power of God himself.

Once upon a time there was a small village deep in the mountains that celebrated Christmas in a unique way. Lovely gifts grew in the forest behind the village. You could pluck beautiful dolls, fully dressed and detailed, from hazel bushes. Walnut trees yielded toys as well as walnuts. The yew provided books and crayons, and so on. The day before Christmas, the village children would go out into the forest to pick out lovely gifts for all their brothers, sisters, parents, and friends.

One Christmas Eve, one of the older children said, "This is ridiculous. When we choose each other's gifts, how do we know what these other people want? Let us each choose our own gifts, then we're all sure of getting exactly what we want. After all, the presents come from the same place."

All the children fell in with the plan, except for one boy. His sister was crippled and unable to clamber through the forest. So he went out with the intention of finding her something especially nice, at the cost of getting anything for himself.

As darkness fell, the other children returned crestfallen. "There are no gifts out there this year," they moaned. "The forests are empty! Nothing! Not even walnuts."

The little boy looked confused. "How can you say that? I found a wonderful present for my sister. The forest was so filled with lovely things, I had trouble choosing."

Looking out for others while God looks out for you fills the forest of your life with lovely things.

Christ Wouldn't Tell You "Think for Yourself"

We Americans don't wear our hearts on our sleeves; we wear them on our bumpers. Bumper stickers never cease to amuse and amaze me.

During the last administration I saw a car that definitely belonged to a Democrat. The bumper sticker said, "I [heart] Barbara Bush," and in tiny print, "Can't stand her husband."

And no doubt from a Republican: "I'm O.K. You're O.K. Clinton's an Okie."

"Cowboy Power!"

"When the going gets tough, the tough go shopping."

"Of all the things I've lost, I miss my mind the most."

"QUESTION REALITY."

That last one reflects another message we get from certain self-help books: that we must decide for ourselves what to think. "Separate from what others believe and examine reality for yourself," these books say. "Believe what you want to believe, and don't let anyone tell you otherwise," they add. Many of these books accept the idea that "As a man thinketh, so is he," but they teach that we should be the ones who decide what to think and what not to think.

I agree that "As a man thinketh, so is he," and that it is dangerous and destructive to let others determine what we think. That is why I tell my clients that it is important to stop allowing their parents, teachers, friends, pastors, and others do their thinking for them. Yet, I never encourage them to think their own thoughts. I encourage them to think God's thoughts.

All kinds of people want to tell you what to think, and some of these people do have some truths figured out that are worth considering. But you don't want to think something just because your favorite author said it was true, or your pastor taught it from the pulpit, or you heard it over the radio from a widely respected person. The bottom line is whether or not God thinks it.

So, while many books would tell you that you need to do your own thinking, I believe Christ would tell you that you need to let God's truth become your thoughts each day. Christ Himself said, "My doctrine is not Mine, but His who sent Me" (John 7:16). Christ thought as God the Father directed Him.

Let God tell you what to think. No one else. His thoughts are the only ones that truly fit reality and make any sense.

Christ Wouldn't Tell You "Grab for the Gusto Now"

It started out as a beer commercial, as so many catchy slogans do. "You only go around once in life, so go for all the gusto you can get." Many self-help books have picked up the concept, often with the same phrasing.

The first part of that statement is true. The Bible says, "It is appointed for men to die once" (Hebrews 9:27). The problem is the second half of the statement. "But after this the judgment."

A lot of modern counsel includes the self-indulgent, pleasure-seeking stance of "Don't let a pleasurable moment pass you by. Seize them all. If it feels good, do it. If it looks good, possess it. If it tastes good, eat it." I once heard a guy in a locker room put it this way: "I'm going to live fast, die young, and leave a good-looking corpse."

I've said it before: your Counselor is no killjoy. But for your own good He would tell us that we need to say "No" to certain earthly pleasures in order to experience life at its best.

Yes, I can go out this very moment and buy almost anything I want, eat whatever I want, and so on. And it would feel good at the moment, that's for sure. But in seeking pleasure for pleasure's sake, I would be doing these things at the expense of pleasing God. Neither would I be doing my body, Christ's temple, any favors. What feels good isn't always what is best. Christ would tell us to choose what is best even if it means not feeling great at that moment because we will ultimately enjoy even greater pleasure. Yet, it isn't easy trying to delay pleasure in a world focused on instant gratification.

I am confident that Christ would tell you that God has placed certain things here on earth for us to enjoy, but only in the context of His plan for our lives. We are to enjoy sex, but only with our marriage partners. We are to enjoy material possessions, but only those that God wants us to have and with an awareness that they are on loan from Him. We are to enjoy food, but in appropriate quantities at appropriate times. I think you get the point.

So, don't listen to the world when it tells you to "grab for all the gusto" you can get your hands on. Doing so will feel good at the time, but it will make you feel horrible later on. Instead, we are to bypass instant gratification and "Lay up for yourselves treasures in heaven" (Matthew 6:20). To turn a phrase around, we are to live slow, die old, and leave a peaceful looking corpse.

Christ Wouldn't Tell You "Be Positive"

An old song goes something like this, "Accentuate the positive, eliminate the negative, and don't mess with Mr. In-between." Understand, I myself don't remember it; I think my grandmother does. Many similar songs were spawned in the dark days of the World Wars, with lyrics like, "Just direct your feet to the sunny side of the street." The purpose of these songs was to lift our hearts during a time of uncertainty and turmoil. With Americans at war in Europe and the Pacific, we could use all the uplifting we could get. It was good for the war cause, you see.

Long after this era, we still have the emphasis of self-help psychologists on positive thinking. This positive thinking movement urges you to let nothing but upbeat, encouraging, self-promotional, and exciting thoughts enter your mind. At all costs, we are told not to let that which is downbeat, discouraging, self-sacrificial or unexciting find a place in our thoughts. You are what you think. Who wants to be a grump?

From what I know of Christ's teachings, I believe that He would not tell you to think positively. I believe He would tell you to think realistically. There's a big, big difference. Christ isn't concerned with whether or not something is positive or negative, He is concerned about its accuracy.

Some realities are negative. War. Famine. Racial conflict. AIDS. Add to the list the things that concern you most. Would our Counselor, the only perfectly honest individual, jump right in there and tell you that you shouldn't see it that way? In this light, the biblical teaching, "Count it all joy," in the first chapter of the book of James, doesn't mean that we are to run from bad feelings. It simply means that no matter how bad things get, God is still God. So, in the face of the worst things life can throw at us, we can realistically be joyful in the sense that God is still in control and going to make everything right some day.

For those in Christ, the overall forest of our lives is positive, but certain trees, like man's inhumanity to man and our tendency to be selfish and self-destructive, are quite negative and need to be seen that way. I believe Christ would tell you to let the negatives in life be negative and the positives in life be positive, and bathe all of them in God's love, mercy, and justice.

Christ, I believe, does not want positive thinkers on His side. I believe He wants realists who see things exactly for what they are. Until we recognize the problems, we cannot get to work on solutions. Until we see injustice for what it is, we will not fight it or forgive it. If we are going to be effective servants doing God's will, we have to see where to serve. Positive thinking as taught in many self-help books isn't very positive.

The deepest thirst in your life is for truth and for the God who is the author of all truth. The counsel God offers is what you really want, not the shallow advice that so many self-help movements, and the books and counseling methods based on them, offer us.

So, the next time you pick up a self-help book, or sit in a counseling session, secular or Christian, take a close look at what is being said. If you hear any of the misguided notions discussed in this chapter, challenge them. That which appeals to the flesh isn't going to bide well with the spirit. Keep in mind that the things that tickle our ears are often the very things that are the most poisonous to our souls.

Caveat emptor!

XV

Do You Want to Get Well?

"When Jesus saw him lying there, and knew that he already had been in that condition a long time, He said to him, 'Do you want to be made well?'"   John 5:6

There are a number of amazing stories about the life of Christ and the wonderful things He did. You know the stories about Him walking on water, feeding five thousand with five loaves of bread and two fish, giving sight to the blind, and bringing the dead back to life. To me, the healing of an invalid at the pool called Bethesda (see John 5) is one of the most amazing stories of all, and not for the reason you might think. Let me explain.

Christ was in Jerusalem for a feast of the Jews, and He came to the pool at Bethesda where great numbers of invalids went for healing. Blind, lame, and paralyzed people would lie near the pool waiting for the waters to stir. Now the waters of the pool would stir at unpredictable times. When the phenomenon occurred, those who were able hurried down into the water as quickly as possible. The lucky ones who made it into the water in time were sometimes healed of their infirmity. Picture a dank, quiet pool, ringed with desperate people in search of healing for bodies riddled with suffering and pain.

One man who laid there had been an invalid for thirty-eight years. Can you imagine suffering from a horrible ailment for thirty-eight years? What incredible despair the man must have felt as he watched years pass with no improvement in his condition. Yet, in spite of almost four decades of suffering, the man continued to lie there by the pool, unable to jump in when the waters stirred, hoping someone would take pity on him and help him get in when the time was right.

Christ came into that heart-wrenching scene of despair and noticed this one man out of the many there. Christ saw him lying by the pool and learned that he had been there for a long time. Christ then went on to ask the invalid a question, a question that I believe is what makes this such an incredible story: "Do you want to get well?"

Can you imagine? What an unbelievable question to ask a man who has suffered for so long! Yet, I think I know the reason He asked it. I have learned to ask the very same question of people who come to see me for counseling. It is a question that often surprises them, and sometimes even insults them. I ask this question in all seriousness because in my work I have learned something that I believe Christ fully understood: Most people don't really want to get well.

HOW MUCH PAIN IS "ENOUGH"?

I have found, time after time in counseling, that when push comes to shove, most of us don't want to do the work entailed in getting better because it is often inherently painful. To avoid the painful, often thankless, difficult task of getting better, we tend to adjust to the pain of staying ill. Not only do we often grow comfortable with our problems and the pain they create, we often want to hang on to our problems for all the benefits that come with them.

Benefits? Yes, benefits. With few exceptions, all personal problems involve payoffs of one kind or another. We psychologists call these secondary gains. Sure, personal problems are painful, but there's an up side; we like the attention from others they bring into our lives, and we like to use our problems as an excuse to quit trying.

There was, for example, a woman we'll call Mary who had suffered from chronic depression since high school. Sometimes she felt better than at other times, but always in the background hung that heavy weight. She married, earned a graduate degree, and bore two children. She worked as a checkout clerk while her husband completed his doctorate. The moment he graduated, she gave up the checkout job and became a housewife. Her husband obtained an assistant professorship in a small college.

The sex stopped first. Mary found herself avoiding the marital union. Before long she came to abhor it. Her husband gave up trying. Her life grew sluggish. She didn't get around to things. She didn't get the Christmas cards out, so he sent their friends postcards. When they took the kids camping, he loaded and unloaded the car, raised and struck the tent, did most of the cooking; she tagged along. Very little interested her. She savored nothing.

Five years into his academic career, her husband found a woman who enjoyed life. Mary moved in with her parents and filed for divorce. Now her mom takes care of the kids while she works as a checkout clerk. She is miserable. She has lost ten years of good living. Mary underwent counseling to restore, in part, what the locusts had eaten; she stuck with it two months and quit.

Why?

Mary got a lot more attention because of her depression than she would have done if she hadn't been depressed. Friends sympathized with the poor struggling housewife whose husband had found someone new. The favorable attention was too hard to give up.

Too, Mary was not held responsible to do what it would take to overcome her problem. Her mom took care of the kids. Her dad changed the oil in her car. Her parents didn't say "Seek help or you're on your own." Her friends didn't genuinely help her undertake the struggle back to wholeness.

Besides, depression is a very difficult condition to work past. Even people who are ambitious in one area of their lives can be incredibly lazy in other areas. The less Mary did, the less she wanted to do. It was a nasty downward spiral. It was not just that it was easier to live day to day in the pit of her depression; she no longer possessed the emotional energy to climb back out. She said repeatedly she wanted to get over this. In actuality, she didn't want to bother.

Mary is typical of many people who undergo counseling.

Christ knew that people often benefit from having problems. He also knew that after suffering for a long time people tend to lose the will to get better. The fact that the man in the story had suffered for thirty-eight years didn't convince Christ that he really wanted help. The man could have been an invalid for eighty-eight years and the question still needed to be asked, "Have you so adjusted to your problem and the benefits that come with it that you no longer really care to get well?" That wasn't an insulting question for Christ to ask. It was a question that showed how well He knew people and their motivations.

Do you want to get well? Have the benefits of being troubled become so comfortable that you don't want to let go of them? Have you adjusted your life to keep your problems alive and well because the pain of moving in a new direction scares you? Not pleasant questions to be asked, I know. Maybe even a little insulting. Yet, if you are really honest with yourself, you, like Mary and like the man at the pool in Bethesda, need to examine these questions closely.

As you read what I am saying in this chapter, you may be feeling somewhat defensive. You may be feeling that I am accusing everyone who struggles with personal problems of not really wanting to get better. I want you to know that I know that isn't true. I have seen countless examples of people who have struggled with great courage to face their problems head on and have, with God's help, overcome them. Among my own clients, I have often seen tremendous courage shown in an effort to get well. Seeing their efforts is a very humbling thing, because I look at my own life and don't always see the same level of endeavor. So, I know there are people who truly want to change, and who give it their all.

But, if you are hearing me say that most people don't really want to get well, you are hearing me correctly. For every person who musters the courage to face problems and actually do what it takes to get better, there are dozens more who don't. Yet, I believe it is the realization that we don't really want to get better that is the starting point for true change. It is by facing the truth, that we don't really want to get well, that we will break through our own denial and have a chance to actually move ahead. As long as we keep comforting ourselves with the thought, not the intention, that we want to change, we will accomplish nothing. Comfort is a great enemy of change.

What did the woman named Mary need? She needed the strength of Jesus because hers was not sufficient. She needed the strength of her parents to say, "You can turn this around. We'll help you all we can, but we're going to quit enabling." Most of all, she needed to start listening to her Counselor. It would not be comfortable, but it would certainly be infinitely rewarding.

We need to get very uncomfortable about our lives. We need to understand that our natural bent is in the direction of self-destruction, not growth. We need to admit that our lives are hopeless if we are left to our own devices. We need to break through the horrible denial we are all in about who we are and consider the direction in which our lives are headed.

Isn't that what Christ came to earth to tell us? Wasn't He trying to say that we were all "terminally ill" and in need of The Great Physician? Wasn't He trying to break through our denial about how self-destructive we are and trying to offer us a way of life that is the only valid one? Wasn't the whole purpose of His life and death to help the sick get well?

Christ, as the ultimate Counselor, was very much focused on cutting through all our defenses and showing us that without Him we were doomed. Without Christ as our Counselor, we are headed on a very fast train to personal ruin. Every piece of His counsel was, and is, designed to help us turn that train around and head it back in the direction of growth and maturity. Go back through each of the things Christ would tell you once again, and look at His counsel from the perspective that it is offered in your best interest.

Christ said to follow Him because following anyone or anything else gets us lost.

Christ said to know who we look like because drawing our self-image from any other source but God poisons our souls and spirits.

Christ said to love our neighbor as ourselves because we grow the most when committed to fostering another's growth, not just our own.

Christ said to clean the inside of the cup because that is the only way to develop true character and avoid a shallow existence.

Christ said to stop fitting in with our culture because our culture is sick, and adapting to it will make us sick, too.

Christ said to get real because wearing masks makes our lives empty and our relationships unfulfilling.

Christ said to stop blaming others because taking responsibility for our own problems is essential for true maturity and health.

Christ said to forgive others because unforgiveness is arrogant and hurts others as well as ourselves.

Christ said to live like an heir because to live like an orphan leads to settling for far too little in life.

Christ said to solve paradoxes because it is often that which seems contrary to common sense that is the healthiest route of all.

Christ said to stop worrying because worry only drains us of the energy we need to work on the things that we can do something about.

Christ said to persevere because the fruit of our labor won't ever show up if we grow tired of doing what it takes to bear it.

Everything Christ tells us is in our best interest, and it is critically important to understand that. His counsel wasn't designed to burden us, but to set us free. When He gave His counsel to us, it was aimed at meeting our deepest needs and it will if we follow it.

When all is said and done, there was one person whose counsel was truly worth listening to and acting on. That person was Jesus

Christ. Before we listen to anyone else's counsel on how to overcome our problems and live life fully, we need to listen to His counsel first. St. Augustine put it this way: "Christ is not valued at all unless he be valued above all." Failure to value Christ above all is failure indeed.

Christ began His efforts to counsel you when He said "Follow me." He finished by encouraging you to "Never quit!" Now, He is asking you "Do you really want to get well?" It is, perhaps, one of the toughest questions any of us will ever be asked. If the answer is "Yes," then Christ is ready, willing, and able to help you. But, there is only one way to prove that you really want to get well—you have to commit your life to Christ and do what He tells you to do each day. Anything less than that won't be enough.

The master plans for an abundant life have been drawn up. They must be followed if our lives are to turn out the way they were meant to. Health in the fullest sense of the word is available to anyone who truly wants it. Christ stands ready to respond to our deepest hurts and needs and to help us find the abundant life we all long for.

Now, answer the question. Do you really want to get well?